Ashley,

My wish for y...

BE THE

BUBBLE

Just remember to be you

Bradley Dean Silberman

Published by TW Publishers
E-mail: hello@twpublishers.co.za
Website: www.twpublishers.co.za
Office: +27647794326 / WhatsApp: +27647794326
47 Thomas Street, Olifantsfontein, 1666
Midrand, South Africa

Disclaimer: The purpose of this book is to educate and entertain. The author and/or publisher do not guarantee that anyone following these techniques, suggestions, tips, ideas, or strategies will become successful. The author and/or publisher shall have neither liability nor responsibility to anyone with respect to any loss or damage caused, or alleged to be caused, directly or indirectly by the information contained in this book.

Typeset in Stix Two Text, 12pts
Paperback ISBN: 978-0-620-95834-9
Kindle ISBN: 978-0-620-95835-6

DEDICATION

This book is dedicated to you!

Specifically, to all the supporters that prayed for me day in and day out. To my family. To my friends. To those that were by my bedside. To those across the world. To the strangers that had me in their thoughts and prayers.

This book is for YOU...

To Be The Bubble

CONTENTS

CONTENTS

INTRODUCTION

In 2004 I was attacked by bouncers outside a club. I was a 22 year old engineering student. The attack, which nearly killed me, made headlines at the time and inspired an outpouring of support from all around the world.

My long road to recovery surprised even my doctors. My neurosurgeon and trauma surgeon didn't have much hope that I'd survive, never mind live a normal, healthy life.

My path to recovery wasn't easy. It was damn tough, actually. But it taught me life-changing lessons. Strange as it sounds, I'm grateful for what happened and the new direction my life took after that incident.

To help me better understand what I was going through, and communicate my story with others, I completed courses in life coaching, mind power and meditation.

More dauntingly, I had to work to overcome my fear of public speaking so that I could share my story.

Speaking to an engaged audience was actually the catalyst for writing this book. I was invited to give a talk by a community leader. He called me a couple of days later to say that everyone had been enrapt - not just with the sometimes sensational details of my personal story but also by the concrete lessons imparted to the audience.

Straight after that call, I opened my diary and set aside time the next morning, a Monday, to try and put my story and my principles into writing. I've managed to fence off a regular session of writing time in the work week, to focus on the project. In retrospect, I realise that the principles I was now living my life by had prompted me to start writing, without waiting for some imagined future moment when I would magically have the time and space to write.

The process of putting these disparate but connected principles into an overall system has proven to be incredibly fruitful, for me as well as those around me. Those around me include family, friends, companies, clients and sales teams.

By writing this book, I have three main purposes: to share these discoveries with everyone who might want to use them; to show how these principles connect and interact with each other; and to show how the principles can connect with and uplift you in every element of life.

Be the Bubble is a concept of mind. It's a technique for anyone at any level of life.

The system consists of 6 interconnected discoveries that, taken together, enable people to live with intention and purpose. That's easy to say in abstract, but my aim is to present concrete, achievable steps to help people achieve defined goals.

The book begins with an account of who I was and who I became. More importantly, it details the steps I took to get from the former to the latter. The narrative explains the discoveries and the discoveries reveal the substance of the narrative.

Today I'm a husband and father with successful businesses. Each business aligns with who I now am. I feel like I make a difference. As I hope the book makes clear, I wouldn't have it any other way.

"Do what you can, with what you have, where you are. It is not the critic who counts; not the man who points out how the strong man stumbles, or where the doer of deeds could have done them better. The credit belongs to the man who is actually in the arena, whose face is marred by dust and sweat and blood; who strives valiantly; who errs, who comes short again and again, because there is no effort without error and shortcoming; but who does actually strive to do the deeds; who knows great enthusiasms, the great devotions; who spends himself in a worthy cause; who at the best knows in the end the triumph of high achievement, and who at the worst, if he fails, at least fails while daring greatly, so that his place shall never be with those cold and timid souls who neither know victory nor defeat."

Theodore Roosevelt

MY NAME IS BEEF

My name is Beef. That's what they call me. My real name is Bradley, but I've been known as Beef since school. It's the name my friends use.

It's not one of those ironic nicknames, like Tiny for a 7 foot athlete. I was the toughest guy in my year, maybe in the whole school. 100+ kilos of brawn and star of the rugby team. I like to think I was a chilled guy, but it's not like anyone was going to start trouble with me. Sure, I had a naughty streak, but it was harmless. I was just messing around.

My school years were good. At least they seemed to be. I did well academically (even if it meant copying my girlfriend's notes) and I was popular.

If I didn't exactly apply myself to my studies, I was doing well enough to satisfy my teachers. I thought I knew what I wanted and I seemed to be well on the way to getting it.

I'm not going to say being a big, tough guy defined me. But it was definitely part of who I was, even if I took it for granted. My personality was formed knowing I never needed to get defensive, that I could walk into a room and dominate it. I wasn't going to be intimidated by a big mouth, even if that mouth was backed up by big fists. People called me Beef, for goodness sake.

And like most young people, I felt invincible.I wouldn't even have been able to imagine that before long I would be utterly helpless. Struggling to walk or write my own name. That I would depend on my mother to drive me to meetings and guide me as I tried to figure out the next phase of my life.

I want to tell you how I finally woke up and saw the world and - much more importantly, saw myself - in a completely new way. How I gained clarity and meaning I didn't even know was missing from a life that seemed satisfying, but I now see was aimless, with no real direction.

Maybe that sounds like a cliche: I was asleep and now I'm awake. A bad thing happened, and I overcame it, and now I'm a better person.

But here's something else I learned: there was nothing inevitable about my breakthrough. Hardship can be the greatest teacher, but you need to be open to the lessons it provides.

I was lucky. My doctors didn't think I would survive, never mind live a full and healthy life. But I was lucky in another way. I was lucky to be surrounded by loving and supportive people who helped me get through the crisis, and I was lucky to get the chance to learn from others and to inspire others in a way that gave me strength and insight. That support was essential for turning what seemed like the end into a whole new beginning.

I wouldn't wish what happened to me on anyone. It was a devastating attack on my physical being that almost left me permanently mentally disabled, or worse.

This book is my attempt to communicate the life-changing insights I've learned as a result of the incident. These life-affirming principles will help anyone become a more insightful, appreciative and effective human being, if they are sufficiently internalised.

My greatest joy these days is to help others learn to see the world as I've learned to see it and to gain more control over the meaning of their lives. I've even had to overcome my terror of public speaking to share my insights with audiences.

But to explain how I acquired these lessons, I need to explain who I was before the incident, and how I gained the insights I did. I must warn you, it won't always be pretty.

"If you are depressed, you are living in the past, if you are anxious, you are living in the future, if you are at peace, you are living in the present."

Lao Tzu

FLASHBACK

Flashback to the early 2000's.

I was an engineering student at Wits University. University life was in many ways a continuation of my school years, not that I was complaining. Life felt good. I still copied my girlfriend's notes (who needed all the fuss of actually going to lectures?) I basically did my engineering degree by correspondence, pretty much showing up for exams.

Why engineering? Why not? I needed something I could do that would take me to where I was expected to go. So I'd enrolled in the same degree my older brother had enrolled in. It's not like I had any clear sense of what I wanted to get out of my university experience.

And it was working out just fine. I was captain of the varsity rugby team. I had good friends. I chased girls. I passed my exams well enough. I did what cool guys did on campus.

After all, I was at university to do what was expected of respectable young people. I just wanted to do the minimum to get the credentials needed to be taken seriously by society and be admired. University was an image management process more than anything else. In fact, when I realised I could get my credentials even sooner by switching to a three year maths BSc, I did that. Why spend any more time than necessary going through the motions?

Who knows where I would've coasted along to, with no real sense of seriousness or purpose, concerned more about image than substance, if I hadn't gone to this hot new club to celebrate a friend's birthday...

It's the night of 13 November 2004.

As I headed out to join my friends, my mom told me to have fun and to watch out for the bouncers. It was a weird thing for her to say. I'd never had trouble with bouncers before. I wasn't looking to start any trouble. And besides, everyone liked me. I was just out looking for a good time. Plus I knew the young woman I was looking to hook up with would be at the club that night, so who cares what else was going on.

It was a good party at first. At least, that's what they tell me. I don't remember much about that night, for reasons that will become obvious, and I've had to piece together the sequence of events based on what my friends have told me.

Students being students, before too long the birthday boy was passed out drunk at the bar. Now, it was perfectly reasonable for the door staff to remove him from the premises, and to ask his friends to

14

go out with him. Any self-respecting club owner would want the staff to deal with patrons in a professional way. Contrary to popular belief, being a good bouncer takes real skill and self-control.

Instead, our group was jostled out of the entrance and thrown out onto the pavement. At this point, my friends assure me, I was standing outside minding my own business. I wasn't even looking at the bouncers. They were hopped up on cocaine and steroids, and they picked me out of the group for some reason and laid into me.

At one point, I literally flew into the air and smashed my head down into the concrete of the curb, like the least amusing cartoon you'll ever see.

My friends immediately knew I was not okay. There was Beef, the toughest guy to take down on the rugby field. If I did go down, I got right back up. In situations like this, I was usually the person who stepped in to calm things down. Now I was sprawled on the pavement, my athlete's body lying helpless and immobile.

Fortunately, my friends immediately sprung into action, heaving my 105kg frame into a car and rushing me to the nearest emergency room. And thank goodness they did, because my situation was even worse than it looked. I was diagnosed with a subdural hematoma, bleeding on the brain, and was placed in an induced coma in preparation for emergency brain surgery. The doctors later told my family that if I'd arrived at the hospital just a few minutes later, I likely would've choked to death on my own vomit.

The surgeon was honest and direct with my family. He told them that if I woke up from surgery - and that was a big if - I would be severely brain damaged. I'd probably spend the rest of my life in care, unable to walk or talk, one half step up from a vegetative state.

My family is Jewish, and when the community found out what happened, they immediately organised prayers at the hospital. I mean that very night! People who woke up to the news rushed straight to the hospital to perform morning prayers on my behalf. By 8am, there were hundreds of people at the hospital praying for my recovery.

The prayers and well wishes weren't limited to my own community. As the news spread, there were reports of people of different faiths and cultures praying for my recovery around the world. My brother had set up a website (this was in the blessed days before social media) and messages of support poured in from all over. It's incredibly moving for me to think about that global outpouring of support now. Of course, at the time I wasn't aware of any of it. Or anything else.

The surgery proceeded without incident, but that was only the first step. My brain was swelling dangerously and if it didn't come down in time, that would be it! The last conscious moment of my life would've been standing around the pavement of a Joburg nightclub with a bunch of aggro bouncers.

For my friends and family, my recovery was now just a waiting game. They kept a constant vigil, which meant someone would be there if I woke up. And eventually I did. The swelling had finally come down from a point at which the herniation was extremely dangerous. Any further swelling would've been fatal.

I opened my still blurry eyes, pipes and tubes going this way and that way. The beeping of monitors. I could just about make out some figures in the room and, with my usual poetic way with words I mumbled, "what the fuck is in my neck?" Not exactly Shakespeare but not bad for a guy with a bleeding brain.

And here's the weird thing ... I felt great. My parents ran into the room when they heard I'd woken up, surprised and confused but delighted, and I absolutely couldn't believe it when they explained what had happened to me. I said it felt like I'd just had the best sleep of my life.

That feeling didn't last. As the next few weeks proceeded, I learned more and more each day just how damaged I was. I was a 22 year old student and I couldn't eat or drink unaided. I couldn't walk or bathe without help. I couldn't even go to the toilet on my own.

My mother would feed me yoghurt - I couldn't even hold the spoon - and it would dribble out of my mouth. My eye was now slanted and I had blurry vision. The eye patch the specialist gave me left me feeling like an invalid pirate.

Here's where I give myself credit. I wasn't actually okay, I was no longer strong, but I *was* brave. And that bravery was going to prove invaluable during a period of struggle in which I realised how much I still had to learn about the world and about my place in it.

"The entire universe is conspiring to give you everything that you want"

Abraham Hicks

BRAIN DAMAGED

So there I was. A 22 year old former university rugby player, being spoon fed my supper by my mom.

Meanwhile, the bureaucracy of life goes on. There was still the matter of my degree. I'd missed my final exams, for obvious reasons. Wits University had granted me credits for most of my subjects, but because I'd switched to a maths major, I was required to write a final exam.

I scheduled a meeting with the Dean of Mathematics to see if the department would grant me a late exam. Sounds simple enough? In my previous life I probably would have relished the chance to try charm the Dean. I probably would have been a little too cocky for my own good.

My new normal was as different as you can imagine. My mom drove me to the meeting. She even sat in to make sure I understood what was happening. The walk from the car to the Dean's office almost wiped me out. A 500m stroll, and I felt like I was trying to climb Mount Everest.

The effort was a reality check. There was no way I was going to be able to write a final year maths exam. Not yet. My neurosurgeon had told me to give my brain a rest, but I'm too much of a 'get-up-and-go' kind of guy to simply lay back and accept that.

There had to be some other way.

So I registered at UNISA - South Africa's largest university and one of the eleven mega-distance teaching universities in the world - to do a degree in entrepreneurship. I had a six month wait before studies commenced. I had my hands full with my multiple therapies, but I had to give myself goals beyond simply recovering.

Instead of waiting for my formal instruction in entrepreneurship, I started businesses.

The first was a massage and healing practice, based in my parents' house.

It's no mystery why I was suddenly interested in the healing power of touch. I was undergoing rigorous physio and rehab, and I was keenly aware of my body's every movement and my slow, incremental progress.

But there was another reason. I knew I had a talent. Everyone always said I had 'magic hands', and people kept begging me to give them a back rub. At every braai, house party or formal function, I'd be forced to spend the afternoon giving my buddies neck massages. Everyone insisting it's their turn for a massage.

It sounds like a pain, but I actually enjoyed being the resident massage guy. And now I started thinking more seriously about healing and how I might actually help people. So I started training formally, taking courses in holistic massage, hot stone massage, Indian head massage, reflexology.

Sounds wholesome enough? Well let me tell you, I saw some things. My first massage course was...a lot.

The course was scheduled for a full weekend. It turned out to be five participants, plus an instructor and a model on whom we were all to practice massaging on. Oh, and we were all naked, apart from a flimsy sarong each.

I will say this about the course: it prepared me for some of the uncomfortable experiences that come with the job. In the subsequent career as a massage therapist, I'd encountered a lot of things. Like beautiful naked clients (a lot more naked than they had been requested to be) who lead me to their bedrooms. Clearly, some people wanted services that went beyond the ones listed on my catalogue.

In the meantime, things were a little more restrained. I was too weak to drive, so all business was conducted at my parents house. But when I could, I hired therapists, beauticians and healers. We went mobile and worked across Gauteng. And the business grew. From starting off doing healing massages in my parents home, I would eventually build up a network of jet-setting international clients who would call me over to their luxurious hotel rooms.

If you're expecting this to be the sex, drugs and rock 'n roll section of the book - sorry to disappoint. I was asked to go 'beyond the call of duty' more times than I ever expected, but I wasn't prepared to risk my reputation or to waste my energy.

But I won't pretend I didn't have a good time. It was an exciting period, with many temptations. The experience taught me to be more adaptable. I learned how to be comfortable in almost any situation.

And, I made good money. It's funny to think that if I'd completed my maths degree and followed a traditional career path, I likely wouldn't have been sitting with hundreds of thousands of rands hidden underneath my bed. That may sound trivial, but it taught me a lesson: I'd been given a second chance and I was flourishing because of it. I also realised that my talent for helping people entailed an obligation: I resolved to work, even in my small way, to make the world a better place.

"You don't have to be great to start, but you have to start to be great"

Zig Ziglar

STUDENT LIFE, TAKE 2

June 2005 came quickly. Before I knew it, I was a student again. I enrolled in just three subjects at first. I didn't want to overtax my brain. Even a couple of minutes of reading was painful. I'd read a few pages of a textbook and feel like I need to sleep for a week.

And it wasn't like I just had my studies to worry about. Somehow, I'd become a public figure. I was interviewed on the radio and I appeared on TV news shows. My picture was splashed across the pages of newspapers and magazines. I was probed by journalists, bombarded with questions to which I tried to give thoughtful answers.

Public recognition brought a new threat. My assailants and their crew were none too happy that I was in the public eye. Journalists who interviewed me received threatening calls. I was followed everywhere I went. Even on my drive to my physical, psychological and neurological therapies, I'd see the same car tracking my journey.

But I pushed on. Studying and running a business at the same time wasn't easy - but this time around, I wasn't all about the easy way. So I started a second business, for my trouble. I imported and distributed Thai fishing pants. It was a pretty successful side hustle to my side hustle.

I was making decent cash and I could put myself through university. I've never held a formal day job since, and it's worked for me. I became an entrepreneur almost by accident.

At the time, though, I wasn't sure what my trajectory was. By this time, the friends who were with me the night I was attacked had finished their studies. A bunch of them had left South Africa. I think they wanted to get as far away from the site of the trauma as they could.

Me - I wasn't sure what was going on. I could only really focus on one thing at a time, whatever was right in front of my nose. So I did that.

Meanwhile the wheels of justice were turning, more or less. The bouncers had come forward and accepted a plea bargain from prosecutors. The plea bargain was effectively an admission of guilt. They received a suspended sentence and a R25 000 fine.

We had been strongly advised to accept the deal by lawyers and senior police. And not just for the obvious reasons. I was told the deal would be the first instance of bouncers involved in this kind of incident facing any kind of justice. The precedent would supposedly help others in similar situations. Incidents like mine were very common, it's just that you rarely hear about them. After all, other victims don't have my mom. After my incident, my mother had called every journalist and radio station. She made sure the whole country knew what had happened, in all its gory detail.

I accepted the deal. What else could I do? I can't exactly say it felt like justice, but nothing was going to feel like real justice.

But here's the real kick in the balls. For the plea bargain to go through, I had to appear in court to agree to it. That meant meeting my assailants for the first time since the assault. Up to that point, I didn't even really know what they looked like. I wasn't sure what they would be like or how they would react in court. But I felt I had no choice but to suck it up and face my fears. In the end, everything went smoothly. I stood up in court and agreed to the deal. They accepted guilt and received their sentence. But it was terrifying and I don't wish the experience on anyone.

The legal journey didn't have to end there, though. We still had the option of filing a civil suit. It was tempting. Why shouldn't they pay for what they did?

Again, the cops and lawyers advised against taking action. We were warned there would be retribution. These were bad guys, they wouldn't take our legal threats lying down. We were warned of a real threat to our safety if we sued.

I didn't want to put my family at risk. And anyway, my priority at the time was to work on recovering. So that was that. I was in rehab and those thugs got a slap on the wrist. But you know what, things always happen for a reason - even if I didn't know what it was yet.

It took a full three years to reach the point where I can say that I was back to 'normal'. I'd recovered enough that I could enter relationships again and interact with my friends like in the old days. I could read a chapter of my textbook without needing to take a nap.

My small-time mobile massage service had grown into a real business. It had transformed into a corporate wellness company. We offered on-site massages and speed manicures and pedicures.

We gained a reputation for good service and started offering more services. Our corporate health portfolio includes wellness programmes, fitness challenges, nutrition advice and sexual health seminars. We even offered educational seminars on substance abuse and gender-based violence. It was quite a leap from healing massages in my parents' home to providing a full suite of corporate wellness services for major firms. We were often the first-to-market, quickly establishing ourselves as market leaders. And to think, I could have landed up doing data entry at some desk job for nine hours a day.

The experience taught me how to be an entrepreneur, but for a surprising reason. I didn't like the direction the industry was taking. I always thought 'wellness' was about helping people, but as often as not, it was an opportunity just to make a quick buck. And that drove me to keep working, to create products and services that were actually aligned to my values. If I was going to operate in the wellness space, I wanted my work to improve people's lives.

That drive stayed with me. I became a serial entrepreneur. Anything that interested me, I worked on turning it into a business. From frozen yoghurt to craft beer to wellness apps, bespoke pharmacy benefits, medical insurance and telcos. I threw myself, with all my energy, at everything and anything.

Entrepreneurship is an attitude as much as anything. I became fearless. I could create a business out of barely anything at all.

And meanwhile ... I graduated. Seven years later, and I had my degree.

Graduation was an eye opener. I was blown away at how proud all the students and parents were. How happy everyone was. During my first go at being a student, I'd taken the opportunity for granted. Graduating with my fellow students, I realised how privileged I was. And how lucky!

"Every human being is the author of his own health or disease."

Gautama Buddha

GUT REACTION

My body has always spoken to me. But I haven't always listened. In particular, my stomach is a kind of messenger. When I get an attack - cramping, diarrhoea, a twisting pain (sorry, but the facts aren't always pretty) - I should know something is going to happen. Probably something fucking crazy. But I had to learn that the hard way.

Once, not that long ago, I was doing some consulting work. It was the first time I was working professionally on a project outside of my calling. During that period, I started experiencing stabbing pains. I've experienced a lot of physical pain in my life, as you might imagine, but this was off the charts.

It turned out to be severe gout. High levels of uric acid were leading to needle-like crystals in my joints. It was excruciating.

I went to a rheumatologist, who put me on chronic meds. I had to go on a special diet.

And on paper, I was getting healthier. My uric acid levels were down. There was no medical reason why I should still experience symptoms.

And yet the pain persisted. I lived with it for nearly two years.

Here's when the pain went away: I made a clear decision to let go of the pain. I decided in no uncertain terms that I'd had enough of the pain. At the same time, I left that consultancy job. It wasn't what I was supposed to be doing.

Making those choices - to resume working for my purpose, and to let go of my pain - was the key to healing myself.

In fact, I recently had a premonition that brought on another attack of gout. At the time I didn't see the connection, but I came to realise that this challenge had entered my life precisely for me to overcome it. That process led me to a powerful new epiphany, but that's a story for another time.

"Forgive but do not forget, or you will be hurt again. Forgiving changes the perspectives. Forgetting loses the lesson."

Paulo Coelho

A CHANCE ENCOUNTER WITH AN OLD FRIEND

Here's an especially dramatic example of what happens when I don't listen to what my gut is telling me.

In 2015, a friend was visiting from abroad. He had tickets for Ultra, the EDM festival.

In the run up to the party, I'd been man down for days. Shivering with a high temperature, muscle aches. On the day, I had terrible stomach problems. I'll spare you the details. I definitely did not feel like partying.

But my buddy wasn't about to take no for an answer. He rocked up at my house and told me to put on a shirt. What was I going to do? He was only in town for a short business trip, so I took a handful of medication and pushed on.

My friend had bought the most expensive tickets. And as it turned out, I was enjoying myself. I was glad I'd gone out. I was in the flow, having a good time, when a mountain-sized man approached me, shook my hand and said, you're Bradley? Yes, that's me. Silberman? Yes, that's definitely me. He introduced himself. Let's call him Andrew.

Andrew? The name didn't ring any immediate bell. "I don't want to cause any trouble, but I'm Andrew Smith." It was the bouncer who had hit me 11 years earlier.

"Listen mate, let me just tell you something..." He held his hand aggressively to my chest, thumping me with the back of his hand. His crew was standing behind him, looking like they wanted to pounce.

Listen, Andrew went on, it wasn't so bad, nothing like the papers suggested. He'd given me a little klap, that's all. No big deal. Actually, he'd saved my life, because he'd helped carry me to the car.

I told him the truth: I don't know exactly what happened because I can't remember any of it. He went on about how the media had ruined his life, he had to take his kids out of private school.

He was macho, aggressive and angry. He seemed to want my sympathy and also to blame me and my family, as if it was somehow my fault that he'd bludgeoned me to the point of brain damage.

And this is how I replied: I said I know what happened although I have no memory of it. And to be honest, I am not interested in what you say now. All I can say is... thank you! Thank you for making me a better man.

Instantly, his aggro energy dropped. He became deflated. I asked him if he knew what I'd been through. How I had to relearn how to walk and talk, how to eat and bath, at age 22. He said he never knew any of that. He stepped up and said sorry and we hugged. If you'd told me a scene like that could happen when I was standing in court, agreeing to that plea deal, I would never have believed it.

You might think this is a story of hope and redemption, of reconciliation against the odds and finding meaning in trauma. And sure, it is. But I want to talk about my stomach.

Because the point is, I had that familiar ache in my guts before the concert. It was a premonition. My stomach was telling me something.

A few years after the incident, I did actually get very ill. I had to go to the toilet 30 times a day. Every joint ached. And it persisted. I'd previously been diagnosed with Crohn's Disease and went to my doctor to try get to the bottom of things, so to speak. He said I was fine. I was actually doing well, the Crohn's was in remission.

That in itself was remarkable because Crohn's doesn't usually go into remission. I was first diagnosed with the disease a year before I was assaulted. That was at the end of 2003. I was attacked at the end of 2004. It was a few years later, after the incident and the long journey of my recovery, that my doctor revealed that my Crohn's was in remission. Was the Crohn's a foreshadowing of the trauma that was to come?

But if I was so healthy, why was I so sick?

I looked for answers outside of Western medicine. Through my journey, I have come to believe that I was so ill because of my unconscious trauma. On a conscious level, I had come to accept that my assault was for that greater good. I had overcome anger and despair. But on a deeper level, I was still tormented. And that trauma was expressed in physical distress.

My first step on the path to greater wellness was a visit to a holistic doctor who assessed me in both standard scientific medical terms and according to the principles of Eastern and other alternative practices.

I was advised to go on a personalised healing diet. I was also told to undergo regression hypnotherapy to help heal the trauma I was holding onto deep inside.

Something profound like that, where you have no control over the journey you take, takes real trust. I found a hypnotherapist I felt a connection to, and after a few consultations, the therapist told me I was ready for hypnosis.

The hypnosis probably lasted a few minutes but it felt like I was under for a lifetime. I went to a place I'd never been before. It was beautiful. I felt happy in a way that I can't quite put into words. I was in a bubble on a cloud where my past, my present and my future culminated in one moment.

Once this blissful moment, seemingly outside of time and space, had passed, I awoke and felt ...Well, I felt disappointed. Worse, I felt hollow. I had entered regression hypnotherapy with this massive expectation that my trauma would instantly dissipate - was I just looking for an easy way out? - And instead of confronting past selves and peering deep into the origins of my being, I was all alone in a bubble (wonderful enchanted bubble, sure) with just myself. And why would I go through all that trouble to hang out with that doofus?

Yes, I'd had a moment of blissful calm inside that bubble, but I wasn't looking for an expensive power nap, I was seeking healing.

And yet, something interesting was happening. My wife was the first to consciously notice. She told me I was calmer and more confident. That I had a much stronger sense of my self-worth and I was acting more decisively.

That confidence was evident in my behaviour. I was taking control and following my passions. I was doing things that I'd always wanted to try, but was held back by doubt or fear. It was an incremental process, but it was real.

Here's one example, a crucial one. From the time that I'd recovered sufficiently, people have asked me to speak publicly about my journey. I always agreed in theory, but couldn't bring myself to follow though. I told myself I wasn't ready, 'the time isn't right' yadda yadda. It was all cheap excuses. The truth is, I was afraid. I had the usual fear of public speaking, but there was also something else: I was afraid I didn't have anything worth saying. My life story was unusual and certainly full of colour, but I was worried it wouldn't inspire anyone or teach people anything new.

My newfound confidence, and my resolve to take action, finally pushed me onto the stage to tell my story.

In 2016, I finally started speaking publicly. Here's my strategy: I walked on stage and said, fuck it, let's go. So what if my stage presence was good or bad, or if I failed to inspire anyone. I had nothing to lose by embracing my fear and summiting that mountain.

Embracing my fear, compelling myself into action - this was a decisive decision that has affected everything I do, from how I run my businesses to the way I engage with family, friends and strangers. It's why I sat down to write this book.

"I learned that courage was not the absence of fear, but the triumph over it. The brave man is not he who does not feel afraid, but he who conquers that fear."

Nelson Mandela

DRAWING COURAGE FROM THE BUBBLE

So what had happened? I'd had a very pleasant but not deeply meaningful experience, you could even call it a mystical experience, and yet something had happened. Something is still happening. But what is it?

My epiphany came during my first speaking tour. I went from being too afraid to even walk on stage to giving fifteen public talks in my first year as a speaker.

Embracing my fear made me think about what value I was offering people - and whether I could do more for people, more sustainably. Those reflections took me back to that bubble on a cloud.

In fact, I had a sudden epiphany in the middle of a public talk. I literally stopped for a moment and basked in a realisation. I felt nothing but contentment for where I was at the moment. I was in a bubble on a cloud where my past, my present and my future culminated in a single moment.

Who was in that cloud? It was just me, but it was me looking at myself. For the first time truly seeing myself naked, in every sense: my whole being, just as I am, defined on my own terms.

We can't usually bring ourselves to see ourselves without defensive filters, unmediated by society's view of ourselves. But in that bubble, it was just me and myself - my true self - and you know what? I loved it. I loved seeing myself as I was, and I trusted myself. I was beautiful, inside and out, and I didn't need any affirmation from outside of myself.

In the bubble, I saw everything I needed to succeed, all the resources I needed. I had to surrender to myself with love and trust. And, at least on some level, I woke up from the bubble with that knowledge intact. It was driving my behaviour. But I only gained conscious recognition when the conditions were right.

I perceived that I was successful right now. I stopped anticipating success that was yet to come. My perception of success acted as a compass, guiding me to what I needed to do here on earth.

My epiphany had a powerful effect. Not just because it helped me channel my insight into more direct action and learning. But because once I understood my insight, I wanted to share it. I wanted to bring others to the same realisation - to bring them into the bubble.

Of course, I had no idea how I was going to do that. People told me that my talks were inspiring, but was inspiration enough?

I knew I had to undergo rigorous training. My intuition was a powerful guide, but I needed a framework to work in. And the guidance of mentors.

I enrolled in life coaching and healing courses. I studied meditation. I worked on creating a blueprint for transforming lives.

"Life is never made unbearable by circumstances, but only by lack of meaning and purpose."

Viktor Frankl

LIFE COACHING

Life coaching was fascinating on an intellectual level, especially the intensive neuroscience module, which formed the basis of the life coaching method. But the experience wasn't all book learning. One incident especially stands out.

There were about thirty of us, gathered at an upmarket hotel conference room. One day, we were handed a jar which contained little strips of paper with all the participants' names. The idea was that we would pick a name out of the jar and then observe that person. At the end of the course, we would say something about the person we had picked and that person would say something about us.

I picked my own name. That was pretty unlikely. In fact, the instructors had never seen it happen before. We all put our names back in the jar, mixed them up, and picked again.

Second attempt. I chose the name of an older man, an experienced life coach who was looking to add some more tools to his life coaching toolbox.

It turned out to be a consequential choice. When the time came for us to stand up and reflect on the other person, it turned out that he had prepared more than a few impromptu comments.

He had written notes. He was the only one to do that. In fact, he had written a full, beautiful letter in which he told the group that I had a rare gift of empathy. An ability to feel what it is like to be another person.

It was an extremely moving and wonderfully written letter. It brought the whole room to tears.

He wrote: "Many people feel at peace being in your presence because your understanding of people goes beyond the words they can find to express themselves."

I was stunned at that line. That was me? People really felt that way when they were with me?

Watching him read that letter about me, all those things he was saying about my abilities and character, a letter that turned a group of adults teary-eyed, was a very poignant experience.

It was also a clarifying one. I was now more certain than ever that I was on the right path. I was following my purpose. I was clear about my talents and I knew I wanted to use them to help people.

Ultimately, we are self-sufficient but we are not for ourselves alone. The course was yet another reminder that I have everything I need to flourish within myself and that once you ground yourself in yourself, your connections with others become more profound and true.

"He who has a why to live for can bear almost any how."

Friedrich Nietzsche

LESSONS

I've told you the story of my life. Not the whole story, of course, but I hope I've conveyed something of the essence of what I've been through.

In my journey, I've made a number of discoveries that have changed my life. Sometimes I didn't even realise I'd made them. I was incorporating insights I'd gained on an unconscious level, and these insights were altering my behaviour in profound ways.

My aim in sharing these discoveries isn't just to give people something interesting to think about. These aren't intellectual exercises, they are a form of practical wisdom for living.

That said, it's fine if nothing changes immediately. When you are ready, these insights will manifest. When you need these insights, they will help you.

In putting these lessons down, I'm trying to help people make sense of intuitions many of us already have. But we don't know how to process them or to put them into action.

As our sense of our self changes, our behaviour starts to change, and new ways of thinking and doing affect the way we see ourselves and the world around us.

It's a very powerful positive feedback loop.

The point is that you don't have to change everything about yourself all at once.

Incremental changes, even apparently trivial ones, can have an extraordinary positive cumulative effect.

Unfortunately, the same is true of negative thoughts and behaviours. I present the following discoveries to help you enter a cycle of positive growth. At the same time, I want to give you tools to disrupt the cycle of distress and negativity that prevents people from being who they want to be (that prevents them from seeing who they truly are).

"The real voyage of discovery consists not in seeking new landscapes, but in having new eyes."

Marcel Proust

DISCOVERIES

Before I outline my discoveries, I want to explain how I've chosen these lessons.

Why these discoveries?

We are all on a journey to find out who we already are. This journey is made up of thousands of complex energies and confusions that push, pull and twist us in all different shapes and sizes - often, ones that we do not want to get caught up in but ones that we struggle to get out of.

Because of this, we often feel unworthy, unloved, not good enough, and wish we were better or did better, or got that job and not this one, or had those type of friends, or had that partner or that house, or that car or that face or body or legs or lips or boobs, vagina or penis.

These thousands of complex energies and confusions - the elements of our lives that make us who we are, that makes us so special and unique - can either break us or serve us.

Because I am the type of person that looks at the meaning, the reason and the purpose of everything that comes my way, good and bad, ugly and gorgeous, and because of my journey of nearly dying, living with brain damage and becoming the man that I was meant to become, I have pinpointed the discoveries of how to live life to its fullest, to understand how to be happy, positive, grateful with a mindset of success through everything that comes your way. From this you can always be who you are with what you have. The journey that you are on will be traveled positively, joyously and successfully.

The discoveries I have pinpointed are the ones that fit best together to fulfill the following objectives:

- o   To live the life you have to its fullest

- o   To live the life that you have for you, because of you, with intention and on purpose

- o   To create success in whatever you touch or look at

- o   To use the tools that you were blessed to receive and to manage your emotions, positive and negative, so that you never lose track of who you are, what you have and where you are going

- o   To control your thoughts, speech and action

Each discovery is a link to the next one, each of which plays a significant part in all of them. They all work together but need to be understood, acknowledged and controlled individually.

You may find elements within each discovery that mean something totally different and unique to you. Your way may be different to mine as well as to any other person. Even so, the discovery counts, so take what counts for you and use it to enhance your world. The principles in this book will allow you to trust yourself and to fly on the wings that you have created.

Often, thoughts, ideas and epiphanies will be released from being the bubble. These may come up immediately or long after you first observed it or after a specific event. This is because there is a link between your conscious self and subconscious self. The link between your subconscious self may take many years to manifest. This may be based on where you are now, how you think, what this means to you and the practicality of using it in your life now; and it might bring up various other ideas and philosophies related to your experience and journey of life years later on.

"A Change of Attitude is a Change of Life"

Bradley Silberman

Discovery 1: Perception VS. Attitude

The most important principle of it all relates to how you engage with reality. This is the first step on the journey to Be the Bubble because it is how you first perceive; the beliefs that you have about yourself and what happens to you and the ones you love.

The key principle to everything in your life is how you perceive it.

The standard definition of perception is:

- become aware or conscious of (something); come to realize or understand

- interpret or regard (someone or something) in a particular way

My interpretation of perception is:

- How I see or view things.

- What I believe.

Perception is the thing that gives rise to an action.

Perception is the cause!

After you see, view or believe something, your behaviour, your actions, your thoughts, your speech, your words and what you do is defined. The ways in which you see, define who you are and what you become, which is the energy you walk with for the rest of your life. Your perception essentially becomes your attitude to yourself, to the ones you love, your teachers, your colleagues, your lovers, your spouse, your pets, your children and everyone and everything around you.

The definition of attitude is:

- a settled way of thinking or feeling about something

My interpretation:

- how I behave / react based on how I see something.

Attitude is an action by which something is achieved. It is a *method*.

Attitude is the means!

To recap: perception is what you see; it is the first step that defines your attitude and the energy that you walk with for the rest of your life. It is the cause which gives rise to an action - your attitude. Perception is what you see and attitude is how you behave because of what you see.

The way they are related is straightforward. Attitude is a direct response to perception.

Once you come to perceive / understand / regard / see / view something in a particular way, then the attitude you maintain is completely aligned to it, and it becomes how you behave. The life you live every single day is based on this process.

For example:

If I perceive / understand / regard / see / view:

Myself as stupid, then my behaviour and attitude is in direct alignment with my view, and so that is how I behave. The energy I walk with and the thoughts that I have every single day has the element of my perception. The result: I will be stupid and never interact with intelligent people, colleagues, or do intelligent things, get that degree or job. I will therefore settle for what I think I am based on the perception that I have.

If I perceive / understand / regard / see / view:

Myself as ugly and/or too fat to get that person, then my behaviour and attitude is in direct alignment with my view and so that is how I behave. The energy I walk with and the thoughts that I have every single day has the element of my perception. The result: I will behave the way I see myself, make no effort to look or feel good and therefore I will not go on a date with that person and so I settle with what I think I can get based on the perception that I have.

If I perceive / understand / regard / see / view:

Myself as too slow, injured, old, and tired to run a marathon, then my behaviour and attitude is in direct alignment with my view and so that is how I behave. The energy I walk with and the thoughts that I have every single day has the element of my perception. The result: I will always be slow, injured, old, tired and unfit to run so I won't run and so I settle with what I think I can't do based on the perception that I have.

If I perceive / understand / regard / see / view:

My car / house as an embarrassment to drive / live in then my behaviour and attitude is in direct alignment with my view and so that is how I behave. The energy I walk with and the thoughts that I have every single day has the element of my perception. The result: I will always be embarrassed, insecure, unworthy, unsuccessful so I settle with what I think I am based on the perception that I have.

The essential point is that once you perceive something, your behaviour and attitude is defined and once you behave in a certain way, you create an energy that sticks with you every step and thought of your way. Your life is then defined by your perception. But you have the control, the responsibility and capability to change it.

The negative perceptions I list above, describe exactly how I felt before my incident. That was my perception. I never knew who I was, how I was feeling, or what I was fighting for. I had no strong

72

sense of where I was going even though I was on the perfect road to success.

I felt lost in the multitudes of energy and I had no purpose, nor worth. I saw myself as fat, unpopular, stupid, incapable and insignificant. I was a victim! I had expectations that did not materialise which made me feel even worse.

Even though my perception was totally inaccurate, something inside me was not satisfied with my lot and although the way I was feeling was my perception and attitude, there was something much deeper than just that. That feeling of unease was there for a reason. It was my gut, my subconscious or connection with the universe that was making me feel that way. I felt dissatisfied because I was on a path that did not align with my purpose and mission. Somewhere deep inside, I knew I was not living my truth nor my purpose.

That feeling is uncomfortable but it is not wrong. It is actually something we should respect, honour and be blessed to feel. We should dig deep to find out the cause and how to utilise it correctly at the right time - that is the means.

For me, the right time was my incident and the realisation I made 12 years later. I have no regrets that it happened or that I did not pick up what I was feeling before. You know why? Because it was meant to be. I am here now, better, stronger, wiser, more connected and frankly sexier than ever!

I actually feel immense gratitude that I underwent my learning experience because I now know my truth. Knowing your truth is something no one can take away from you. This is how you get onto the platform of success. Not anyone else's, but yours. That is where you gain the happiness you seek.

Most of all, I'm grateful that I am able to teach these discoveries to others, so that anyone can live according to Be the Bubble principles.

Let's get deeper into our analysis of perception. I believe that there are generally two perceptions of your life.

1. The world's perception: how the world around you sees you
    o   This is how the world sees you

    o   The world sees the mask that you are wearing

    o   This is how you think you should succeed and it defines the choices you make.

    o   Although it has a huge impact and affect on your perception it is not something you can connect to, as it is not you!

    o   Often you live like this because this is how you see yourself.

    o   When you look at yourself in the mirror, you see the mask you wear and not who you really are.

o   The mask that you are wearing is the mask that you have chosen to wear, which covers not only your face but who and what you are: your behavior, your thoughts, your speech, your words, your actions.

o   This is generally inaccurate, not because it is wrong but because it is not you. It is not your truth. It is what people see: the bullshit you choose as the mask that satisfies the world around you.

2.   Your naked perception: how your purpose sees you

o   This is the perception that is your truth - your nudity!

o   This is you irrespective of what you think the world wants from you or sees from you but how you choose to live - for you!

o   This perception is hard to find and live by but once found is one you will never depart from.

o   This has focus, direction and passion

o   This is what makes you tick

o   This is what makes you free

o   This is what makes you happy

o   This is what makes you feel alive

The perception of my life before the incident was the world's perception. Everything appeared great because everything was measured against those around me and how good or bad they were compared to me. It was not measured according to me and what I am truly capable of: it was measured against my mask!

That perception affected me greatly before the incident. It made me choose my life's path which did not align with my purpose: hence my bad attitude.

You have the power, capability and control to remove that mask, make your own choices, live the life that makes you happy and be who you are.

My discovery showed this to me. When I look back during my recovery, one characteristic that I had stands out most for me. This characteristic, I believe, is one of the three elements that was responsible for my recovery and for me living the way in which I do today. This was the perception I had and the direct response to it: my attitude. This perception was my naked perception and it correlated to the attitude that I had then and to this day - it was one of optimistic acceptance. I accepted the Mount Everest in front of me. I did this because I had no other option except to mount it. There was no room for any negative thoughts, words, nor actions. My perception and attitude were living in symbiosis.

I never experienced hatred towards the thugs who had nearly killed me or put me in a wheelchair for the rest of life. There was never a moment that I wanted them to pay for my suffering. I had no judgement against them. I never asked questions like 'Why me?'. I just took the drama as it came, with an inner realisation that what happened was meant to be, in order for me to be the best that I could be.

I had a pure trust that the universe was giving me a message. The message was for me to enhance myself and elevate the world around me. There was and still is not one piece of negativity and sadness about what I went through. It is actually the total opposite because without it, I would not be here right now with what I have got.

For a number of years before my defining moment, I was that leaf drifting in the middle of the deep blue Atlantic Ocean, where the water was a mix of hot, warm and freezing. The tides would take me wherever it had to go.

We can compare the tides that directed me to the influence of society. What society deemed as cool, happy and successful was my journey. I had no other concept of who I was, who I wanted to be, or my journey ahead.

I was passionate about rugby and the women but I never tried, not even by lifting my left pinky toe, to achieve anything because I was that leaf, directed by the tides/society, staying above the water most of the time. I was comfortable! I was floating successfully!

The point here is that I was comfortable, irrespective of the quality of my days, hot, cold or stormy.

I had comfort because I was wearing my mask. My perception was the world's perception.

Irrespective of where you are in life - your location, social success or whatever, the world's perception and the mask you are wearing will make you feel lonely, inadequate, unworthy and unloved. You will feel like a victim.

When you are a victim, everyone and everything is against you. You are at war every moment of your life. This war is not meaningful to you or to anyone around you. You have created conflict and you are fighting. The question is, what are you fighting for? The answer is absolutely nothing! You are wasting your time, your energy, your effort and missing all the opportunities that surround you every single day.

The defining moment for me was the incident that occurred in 2004. Although it took me 12 years to realise my purpose, the incident provided a realisation that the universe communicates with us and pushes us to do what we are meant to do in order to grow and live life with purpose.

These messages often come with unpleasant moments because we do not hear them the rest of the time, as we are too busy doing what we are doing: fighting a pointless war with no end result except self destruction.

I realised I had a power that only I was responsible for. This power, that I controlled, was the reason why I recovered in a way that was beyond anyone's imagination or expectation. I say power because that is what your perception and attitude can create. It is a form of magic that can take you wherever you need to go.

Through my discovery I coined the term "A Change of Attitude is a Change of Life".

Although I felt lonely, unloved and insignificant before my incident, one of the major reasons I recovered miraculously was because of the power of prayer. The fact that I had so many people around the world praying for my recovery, for my return to the world, and that thousands of people pouring out their love and energy for me, is because I was worthy, significant and loved. No one in the world wanted me to leave them and everyone pleaded with the Almighty to save me. This shifted my perception from the world's perception to my naked perception.

When it comes to perception, forget the negatives. Don't waste your time on unproductive thoughts. Rather, assess why you are viewing what you are viewing, in the way that you are viewing it, and what you can change to benefit your life.

Analyse your path and the direction you are currently in. It is your choice and you can change it. Nothing is fixed. There might be something better for you, a different and more joyful path to follow. Do this with an attitude of optimism because this is happening to uplift you - not to take you down! Trust that the universe is pushing you to be a better you, to make your world a better place. The reason you are shifting is not important. The fact that you are is what matters! Start appreciating who you are, what you have, and your achievements. Stop drifting in the ocean. Remove your mask and focus on your path, what you want to do and how to do it.

We all fall. It's not about the falling but about how we get up. I should know.

Any perception of a negative circumstance can be transformed into a positive action. You need to look at the situation from a different angle.

What is the first step to doing this?

Change your perception and your attitude will follow suit! You have to want to see the situation from a different angle in order to achieve optimism. A change of attitude can be a change of life because once your attitude is changed from your new perception, you can see a variety of paths to follow of a specific "negative" event. Once you have observed the correct path for you, motivation and passion kicks in and nothing will stop you, because you now have the perception, the behaviour and the attitude for success - the perfect ingredients for happiness!

"Your task is not to seek for love, but merely to seek and find all the barriers within yourself that you have built against it."

Rumi

Discovery 2: Love Yourself First

Once you have internalised Discovery 1, you start to see the world around you, including yourself, for what it really is. You have a non-judgemental observation about the world around you - and, crucially, you become non-judgmental about yourself.

When you love yourself enough you are content with your lot. That's because whatever you face from this point on will never overcome the love that you have.

Whatever happens, you have and love yourself. Yes, breakups, divorces, marital affairs, pain, hurt, bad business decisions and losses will still happen. Life won't suddenly become painless. But your love for yourself will lead you, so that you will never disrespect yourself or devalue who you are.

How you love yourself is how you teach others to love and treat you. It defines what you tolerate from the world around you. Your decisions will be for you and not against you.

Enduring hardship will only make the love you have for yourself stronger and better. You will never be the victim but always the victor because whatever you go through will fuel the love that you have for yourself and motivate you to understand that this is all happening for you and not against you.

Put this book down and go right now to look at yourself in the mirror. I don't care where you are. Just go! Look into your eyes, at your face and your body. Have a moment and just look. Now, remove your clothing and look again if you dare. When you come back, I want you to have an answer to the following:

- What do you see?

- Who do you see?

I'm willing to put money down that you did not see who and what you are. You probably have no clue. I'll go double or nothing that you didn't get naked! There's not a chance that you did!

Now, the question is why? Not why don't you know who and what you are? Not why can't you stand a moment with your naked form? The real question to ask is: why aren't you living your best life?

The premise behind loving yourself first is that at any moment in time, under any circumstances, you know one thing: you know who you are and you love it.

Because you know who you are, you are happy. You are confident. You have trust in the resources you have. When you know who you are, your purpose becomes your priority. And living life with purpose is not only good for you, it benefits everyone around you.

When you live with this energy, nothing will compromise your day and your life. It becomes an awareness and understanding that this is your journey and whatever happens is meant to happen. You will always be and do you. You will give or choose not to give because that is who you are and what you do, not because another person gives back to you. You do not need anything from anyone and because of this you will always be yourself.

Your behaviour will not be guided by a desire to receive something or because of some outside cause. Perhaps you always call someone on their birthday and they always forget, but you keep on being you. They probably forget because that is just who they are and you never forget because that is who you are.

When you succumb to other people then you give your power away. In reality, you do not need anything from anyone except yourself. And when you love yourself first is when you keep on doing you!

Does that sound too self-centred? In fact, loving yourself first does not mean not loving other people. It doesn't mean not loving your children or family or partner. Loving yourself in this sense has no arrogance nor ego and does not mean that you put yourself first.

Instead, it does allow you to rather love for the reasons that align with who you are. You do not love to receive. You do not love for other people or to achieve goals. The love you have for anything or anyone is simply love. You love to love and that love gives you even more love for yourself, from yourself, and from and for everyone around you. This is what authentic love is about.

The unloving self is a product of the world around you. It's how you have been guided or mentored by all the people in your life, including your parents, siblings, teachers, friends, colleagues and mentors. It comes from their love for you - but it is not based on what is right for you. It is based on what they think is right for you, in alignment to the world around them. That is the world's perception and not the naked one.

Consequently, you measure yourself against everyone around you. You feel insignificant. You feel like crap.

You create expectations based on what you think you deserve; when those expectations do not materialise you get hurt.

"I am not as pretty or as thin or as rich as them." What does this actually mean to you and to those that you love? It means absolutely nothing. You are the cause of your own disapproval.

Those who truly love you, love you because of exactly what and who you are. Imagine the love they will have for you and the love that you will feel if you began to love yourself. All the love and all the things around you will be enhanced.

Not because of anything else which has no reference to anything you actually "crave". The things you crave for, just frustrate you. Failure to achieve them leads you to doubt your own worth.

Why do you "crave" putting yourself down? You do it because you think that the things you crave will make you feel happier and more worthy. To put it bluntly, that is bullshit.

Only loving yourself first will make you better, make you happier, make you feel the worth that you desire. You will feel and be significant, feel confident and loved - *not* because you achieved something *but simply because of you.*

"I have realized that the past and future are real illusions, that they exist in the present, which is what there is and all there is."

Alan Wilson Watts

Discovery 3: Realistic Illusions

Once you love yourself you can finally appreciate that there is no such thing as a mistake. Failure does not exist. So then what are you scared of?

Yes, fear protects you on the mere plane of survival. But the very same fear is preventing you from fully living.

Stop hating yourself because you should have, could have, and didn't. Stop fearing all those imagined bad things that could happen to you or those you love. That fear is self-destruction.

The irony is that your fear is manifesting those things you are so afraid of. It's bringing your fears to being. Focus on what you want, with love and clarity.

It's simple enough to appreciate in theory that your past has happened for a reason. That there is a purpose. It's much harder to understand that even your perception of your failures exists for that purpose. The person who worries about their past mistakes and missteps? That's you. Love that person and recognise that your fear and regret is an intrinsic stepping stone to a life without fear.

Your past, and all your regrets - that's all you. And you are amazing. At each moment you used your resources and intuitions to make decisions and, you know what, those were the right decisions. Those decisions brought you to this moment, a moment when you choose to embrace yourself in totality and turn your life lessons into a new way of being.

How do you know your achievement today will turn out to be an achievement in years to come? Why are you so sure today's 'failure' will still look like a failure in the future? Everything leads to something. And that something is created by you. Often your biggest 'failures' turn into your life's biggest achievements. Everything we feel and do at every moment is part of the labyrinth of lessons that is life.

So embrace your past. It has given you everything you need to elevate your body, mind and soul. Those bad decisions had reason, meaning and a purpose and right now you are here ready to kick some ass to become who you have always been.

And here's how you do it. To many of you, this may sound counterintuitive. The secret is to stop searching for yourself!

You're right here. It's time to stop searching and start living.

The perception of your supposed mistakes or failures are the building blocks on which to build your new life. This is the biggest learning of your life so appreciate the education of your journey.

Breaking the fear cycle

There is, however, one failure that is real. We've all made it. It's the failure of being afraid. We grow up with this fear, and unless we actively work to break free from it, we can live with it our whole lives.

This fear defines our whole lives, it controls us. Specifically, I'm talking about the fear of failure.

You are scared because you think you aren't good enough and that fear stops you from being yourself and living for yourself! Fear actually crushes all the previous discoveries - your perceptions, your attitudes, your love for yourself and the world around you! Because of this, every second of your life you are failing yourself and the world around you!

To understand fear and where it originates, let's take a look at the words originating from the definition of fear itself, and analyse how they realise themselves in the world. I call this a definition cycle flow. In this case, the definition cycle flow reveals how our beliefs, our existence and our purpose all originate from fear:

Term	Definition
Fear	An unpleasant emotion caused by the **threat** of danger, pain, or harm
Threat	The **possibility** of trouble, danger, or ruin

Possibility	A thing that may be chosen or done out of several possible **alternatives**
Alternatives	(of one or more things) available as another possibility or **choice**
Choice	The **act** of choosing
Act	Do or **create** something
Create	Bring into **existence**
Existence	A way of living and **belief** system
Belief	An **acceptance** that something exists or is true, especially one without proof.
Acceptance	Agreement with or belief in an **idea** or explanation
Idea	The aim or **purpose**
Purpose	The reason for which something is done or created or for which something exists

We define our lives, measure ourselves, choose our perceptions, maintain our attitudes, create the fear we have and simply exist on a false idea or belief system which is in fact the definition of an **illusion**. Let's continue with the definition cycle flow for illusion:

Term	**Definition**
Illusion	A **false** idea or belief
False	Made to imitate something in order to **deceive**
Deceive	Fail to admit to oneself that something is true

Can you see it?

We are actually deceiving ourselves by holding onto fear. The deceit is through being afraid; we are human after all. The deceit comes when we give fear the power to define who we are, what we want and how we live.

We all feel fear but we have to learn to acknowledge that fear is a gift that provides us with tools to grow.

Fear holds us back. Fear prevents our individual genius from coming out and playing. Fear is at the forefront of everything we choose to do and it prevents us from doing epic things, or the things that we need to do, big or small. Fear stops us in our tracks to live life for us and on purpose!

We can only be truly successful if we are willing to fail because failing provides building blocks to step up. If we are unwilling to fail then we are unwilling to succeed. For this reason we need to face our fears, which are our individual stepping stones for us to grow and create success. It's time to step up and live.

We all live with a sense of inadequacy and unworthiness because of our failures, mistakes and how we compare ourselves to the world around us. We are stuck with this failure blockage because of the fear that we hold within us.

This blockage is what causes us to be average and mediocre. Because of fear, you fail to transform into the person you are meant to be. Because of fear you fail to perceive you and your life the way you should and therefore you don't love yourself like you should.

You can't just wave fear away or pretend it doesn't exist. You need to disrupt that fear through conscious action. When you perceive something as a mistake or failure, rather consider the following:

- There is no such thing as failure.

- What we think is failure or mistakes are actually lessons that stretch and push us to be who we are meant to be and successful.

- We can only succeed if we face our fears with the acceptance that failure or the mistakes we make are our building blocks enabling us to reach our maximum capacities.

- When we make mistakes or experience "failure", we should be grateful because the universe is showing us how to grow and succeed by putting stepping stones right in front of our feet.

- When you think you fail is when you become uncomfortable. You only grow from being uncomfortable. Stepping up is being uncomfortable. It is using your strength, your might and your courage to grow. Be uncomfortable and tackle what you need to.

"We are shaped by our thoughts; we become what we think. When the mind is pure, joy follows like a shadow that never leaves"

Buddha

Discovery 4: It's all about choices

Up to this point, this book has been designed to give you the tools and resources you need to transform yourself into the person you have always wanted to be - the person you are right now.

What you do with those resources is up to you. You need to choose.

Your whole life is all about choices. Whatever you have been through, what you are going through right now and what is to come all starts with your choice.

Now that you are aware that you have never failed nor made any real mistakes, you can clearly make the correct choice every time you have to. You are ready to understand the choices you make, what happens because of your choices, and what consequences are really about. You have the ability to be mindful about the choices you make and how they can show you which path to take.

But what is a choice?

We all know what the basic act of choosing is, but do we really understand how the consequences of any given affect every other choice. I like to say that each choice affects the digestion of your life.

Why digestion? When a choice is made (or not made), it may seem like a simple and easy process, but it has a lasting effect. Digestion is the process of breaking down food into nutrients, which the body uses for energy, growth and cell repair. Food and drink must be changed into smaller molecules of nutrients before the blood absorbs them and carries them to cells throughout the body. This is an important part of life. Some choices even directly affect digestion: do I feel like a chocolate bar or a sugar free, gluten free, vegan snack? Do I order the burger or the steak or the grilled chicken salad with avo?

Or do I call my buddy Jason or do I select Emily when I feel like having a quick chat? Do I not return that call? Do I say yes or no? Do you go for a run or walk or wait until next week, because next week you will feel more ready, you are getting new socks on the weekend that will make your jog easier.

Do you put a smile or frown on your face when someone cuts you off in traffic or you miss making that big sale. Each seemingly insignificant choice can affect your life forever because all of them have a consequence.

The choices that seem most to affect your life are also the ones that appear to take up most of your thoughts, your mind, your actions and your time. What to study, which person to marry, when to have kids or to not have kids, what job to take or to not take, which business to start.

These choices are harder to make because it is clear that these will change your life; but irrespective of what choice you have to make, it is all confusing at the moment you have to decide.

Choices are not just alone in your head but they are mixed with everyone else's choices, what they think, the world's perception, the expectations of yourself and the world around you and all the bullshit that surrounds you each day.

How the hell are you supposed to know who you are when you cannot make a choice for yourself? Choices are hard to make; ultimately, choose because you have to, and you choose based on what you think is correct. Usually, the decision comes down to the world's perception and not your naked one.

Mindful decision-making

When a choice flows from you and through you. That's where you want to be, because this is the time that you connect to the decisions that you make and pave the road on your journey. Each decision sets you on a path.

When you have your perception vs attitude in check, the love you have for yourself, the acknowledgement that everything that you have experienced, good, bad, ugly or gorgeous was meant to be there, then you will have the power to make the correct decisions that will pave your road to create your journey of living your destiny now. Not in the future. Now!

I have made countless 'incorrect' choices but because I have Be the Bubble in my toolbox I am grateful for every one of them. Each 'mistake' has given me countless stepping stones to summit my mountain. The mountain that I am climbing every single moment of every day of my life.

Although there are bad or incorrect choices, all of them are meant to be there for one reason, which is for you to make the correct ones. From learning from the incorrect choices, for you to put the journey of your life with all the pieces, twists, drama and turns, in acknowledgement, understanding and acceptance so that you can live with the happiness you want and deserve and for you to be successful for you!

For you because no one else matters. When you surrender to yourself you become vulnerable to the decisions you make and live with and you have a sense of insightfulness that makes your choices free flowing and easy. When you have to make a decision in life there are often many options and choices to choose from. When it becomes a clear decision to make based on who you are, what you want, and where you are going, then that is the choice to make. If you know who you are with all the discoveries in check, the choices you make should be comfortable, simple and easy.

What is a consequence?

The dictionary does not provide an adequate understanding of the word 'consequence' in a practical sense of the word, so I look to

104

physics which gives it the energy that we need so we can be mindful about it every step of the way. The deeper and more raw something is, the more we connect to it, be mindful about it and can live our life as such.

The dictionary states that a consequence is a result or effect of an action or condition.

In physics, there are two laws I would like to bring up:

1. For every action, there is an equal and opposite reaction - Isaac Newton's third law of motion

2. Energy is neither created nor destroyed - Julius Robert Mayer's law of conservation of energy

These two laws explain what a consequence actually is in a practical sense of the word.

If we combine the dictionary definition with the laws of physics we see that everything you ever do in your life has a consequence/result/reaction/energy. Once created, that energy is infinite! It will change or transform as it moves but it will never disappear.

Everything, every single thing, is just energy. You, me, the shoes you are wearing, the gel or wax in your hair, your underwear, the chair you are sitting on, the light bulb, the mountain, your brain, your choices, thoughts and what you are thinking right now and even the things you are not - everything!

Energy also has the potential for causing change so even when we create something that we do not want, we have the power and control to transform it into something positive - something that we do want!

The energy created by just a thought, a word, an action, a non-action - even an excuse! - irrespective of how it is created or by what or whom, is always in existence. Good, bad, ugly or gorgeous. It may change direction, paths, and even states but once created it's always there, in your lifetime, your kids' lifetimes and the lifetime to come.

Let's look at the action of speaking or shouting in the tone of your choosing.

Once the action is activated (for example, we speak), an energy is created and can be transformed into another phase/state which could be another thought or emotion for ourselves or a thought or emotion of another person which will again be transformed with additional perceptions and attitudes and cause additional energies/ actions/reactions/consequences/results that may transform into additional phases or states and this will just continue into infinitum. So in simple terms, the energy that you create, irrespective of how you create it - thought, speech or action, causes a cycle that continues and continues and continues and continues and continues and continues and continues and continues... forever, which will pick up other energies/emotions/actions/reactions from other people, phases, thoughts, words, language or actions...forever!

By talking badly or negatively to yourself, your dog, your competitor, your enemy or someone else creates an infinite bad and negative energy. Let's look at the process of just you for a moment.

Once the thought is created, the emotion is created and the energy of this bad or negative is created. This energy sits within you, even when dormant and is continuously activated whenever another energy stimulates it but it's always within you. Whenever it's activated you create an action which energizes this energy and builds a cycle of negativity which causes a field of self destruction.

Moving onto the next person or group of people, this energy passes this on to the next person, child, student, mother, friend, colleague, enemy, whoever... This energy will then be transformed into another negative/bad energy but it will be slightly different based on the perception, intention, expectation, reaction and energy of whoever takes it on. This again will be within that person or groups of people forever and even when dormant will be activated when something triggers it, just like a volcano and again an action will be created which will pass on this negative energy to the next group of people or things.

The negative energy transfer of negative energy creates many different fields of negative energy created by different perceptions, expectations, intentions and energies of different people or things. The summation of this negative is incalculable but you wouldn't want to be around or live in it but... YOU DO! You not only do but you are one of the creators of it. Well done!

Thinking bad creates bad. Thinking sad creates sadness. Thinking failure creates failure. Thinking unworthiness creates unworthiness.

But...

Thinking good creates good. Thinking happy creates happiness. Thinking success creates success. Thinking worthiness creates worthiness.

So when you tell yourself you are an idiot, guess what? You are an idiot. Not just now but from this point until forever. Once you are an idiot you continue creating idiots by continually being an idiot, making everything in your path idiots and by them making everyone in their paths idiots.

You get yourself into a pattern by thinking and saying and acting the same way and the only way out of it is to control and change your thoughts, your speech and your actions.

By transferring your previously negative thought into a positive thought and action you start transforming your energy into light.

In simple terms:

- whatever you ever do is a real force!

- whatever you ever don't do is a real force!

Let's look at the consequence of not doing something.

The mere act of not acting creates nothing - but this nothing has a consequence. The cycle is created when you do not do something, just like when you do something, irrespective of if this something is a thought, an expectation, a perception, a word or an action.

If you never had the balls to go up to that pretty lady at the bar 20 years ago - non action - then you would have not paved the journey of your current life which is:

- Being young lovers in the night with your soulmate.

- Having a beautiful wedding.

- Becoming parents to three beautiful healthy children. Two boys and one girl.

- Building life long friends for you and your family.

- Meeting that father of your first child's friend at his nursery school who invested in your startup business to create a global disrupter billion dollar company.

- A happy, rewarding and successful life that you have right now.

Now, maybe you would have met another partner in life, had another beautiful wedding, had other kids with different genes, met that investor or another one somewhere else but the point is that a non action can have a multitude of consequences.

Maybe one could have been that you never met your soulmate or got married. Never had kids, had the support of your wife and wife's family to start your business and therefore your life would be totally different. Not worse nor better but different. Remember that wherever you are right now, irrespective of your choices and consequences, is where you are meant to be.

You have everything you need right now to do what you need to do.

If I'd never gone to that club I would have probably qualified as a mathematician and had a career working for someone as a banker. FML!

I am not saying that mathematicians hate their lives but I certainly would have. If I had listened to my gut before I went into that club, I would not have experienced my life's journey the way that I have. I probably would not have married my soulmate and had two beautiful children. I would have never made these discoveries. And we, you and I, would never have shared an energy just like we are experiencing right now: you reading my words and having thoughts about your life and the world around you.

On a deeper level, the consequences of your every action and inaction define your roadmap.

From this you realise that the people in your life, friends, strangers, lovers, family, enemies, ex partners, the ones you have or had an affair with or even nearly, the person you had eye contact with at the grocery store or the person who pulled a middle finger at you, everyone come and gone who you have ever had a moment with has actually created an energy in your life that once has taken place has caused this cycle of infinitum - a consequence which has the power which make you who you are today and defines your journey. Be grateful to all that you have experienced and everyone that has helped you become you.

The bottom line is that although the consequence defines your journey, you have the magic that creates and controls it. The choice is always yours. The way you perceive things.

Your energy builds a force within and around you that makes you who you are, determines what you need and defines your actions.

You may find that you become more open, with the correct priorities in place and more focus. You will feel more from your gut; living a more intuitive life.

By contrast, when you expect something it never meets your perception and therefore always let's you down. In my case, the creation of Be the Bubble was delayed because of the expectation that I had about what I would experience during the regression under hypnotherapy, even though it was all meant to happen.

If you expect A and A occurs then A is generally not as good or bad as the expectation you had. The expectation of a good thing is always better than reality and the reality of a bad thing rarely turns out to be as bad as it was in your head.

Often when I do not feel like going to a celebration and I go, I have the best time. It's the same for anything you experience. An expectation is like your best friend always letting you down, not having your back and lying to you.

Another benefit of no expectations is the sense of randomness. Your life becomes exciting. It becomes non-judgemental. With the Be the Bubble mindset, you can now face anything that comes your way for the purpose of your happiness and success.

Here's a personal story about consequences:

Remember that bouncer who I met for the second time at Ultra?

A year after I met him for the second time, he was involved in an accident and he had to amputate his right arm. This is the arm that he used to beat up, bully and possibly kill hundreds of people in his life.

A year later he was shot and killed by someone similar to who he was.

I am not happy that this happened to him.

Who am I to feel joy for someone else's loss?

Who am I to judge what should happen or happens?

The purpose of me mentioning it here is simply to illustrate what choices and consequences can bring to your life. Anything can happen to anyone at any time. Your energy and actions define what happens to you and you are the only person that is responsible for it occurring.

"If I am not for myself, who will be for me? If I am not for others, what am I? And if not now, when?"

Rabbi Hillel

Discovery 5: Be the Bubble

We are here! At the reason, meaning and purpose of this book.

Be the Bubble is the culmination of it all and allows you to activate your unique reason, meaning and purpose to whatever you are doing, and to live life for you in a happy and successful manner.

When you Be the Bubble, your perception, attitude, love for yourself, management of fear, the choices you make, your decisions and the consequences you create and live with are all perfectly in alignment for you and the world you are living in.

I know that this term sounds crazy - how can you be the bubble? You are not made of a thin sphere of liquid enclosing air or another gas. I chose it because it was my epiphany which painted a vivid vision of how I should live my life purposefully. Now I want to help you mind-shift to a level of awareness, confidence and focus so that you can live a life full of happiness and success.

How do the discoveries prior to this allow you to Be the Bubble?

The way you perceive things to be defines your behaviour and your attitude. Your behaviour stems from this. You will have an objective vision without emotion, fear or any negativity taking your lead.

When you love yourself first, you will feel the worth and significance from deep within your core.

You get what you feel you deserve so that your perception and attitude is always for you and not against you. You become the victor and not the victim and when you embrace your fear and acknowledge that you have never failed but only succeeded, because you are here, you summit your mountain every time you have to, so that you can make the best decisions on the next move.

The choices you make become instinctual, bold and clear. You connect to your intuition and the consequences that you create, by being mindful about what you think, what you say and what you do, are the consequences that you want. You start noticing more than you used to in your daily life. You start seeing the messages, the connections, when to stop and when to move. The road becomes clear and your destiny is not some wish for the future but it is living in this present moment. You become confident, free, happy, alive and successful!

How do we Be the Bubble?

Our lives are made up of the past, the present and the future. We have to deal with all three elements as much as we can so that we can live and have the best day every day.

Because of these three elements, there are three methods to keep in your tool box. These methods are light-weight, with a heavy-weight uppercut, because they are easy to keep on you everyday and are easy to use. Simply put, we need to live in the present, plan for the future ... and fuck the past! We use these methods by first making sure that all the prior discoveries are understood, acknowledged, in alignment with who you are, why you are here and where you are going.

"That is why it is so important to let certain things go. To release them. To cut loose. People need to understand that no one is playing with marked cards; sometimes we win and sometimes we lose. Don't expect to get anything back, don't expect recognition for your efforts, don't expect your genius to be discovered or your love to be understood. Complete the circle. Not out of pride, inability or arrogance, but simply because whatever it is no longer fits in your life. Close the door, change the record, clean the house, get rid of the dust. Stop being who you were and become who you are."

Paulo Coelho

Method 1: Letting Go

Method 1 helps you deal with your past so that you can let go and be present and in the moment to live your destiny.

So how do we let go?

You have to forgive! Forgive every single thing and person that has not put a smile on your face.

There are certain people, memories, incidents and things in our lives that we cannot forget. We harbour them and they affect who we are now. They create blockages that prevent what we should see, use and create. Everyone you remember that hurt you must be forgiven. Whatever they did, whatever the amount of pain you experienced must be let go.

We do this by acknowledging that everything happens for a reason that is derived from love. For a purpose to provide you with the building blocks to build, learn, climb and grow.

Your experience is a direct message from the universe. It is a message of love. You have not become the victim but rather a blessed being. Your experience has been orchestrated from a higher power that has given you an opportunity to learn, build, grow and become the shining light you are meant to be.

For this reason, we know that whatever we are going through, we can overcome. The universe will never put you through something that you cannot handle. At times, it seems really hard and dark. Remember that if there was no dark then there would be no light. This "dark" period is there for you to see the light at the end of the tunnel and to shine with it. This dark period must be seen as a blessing given to you by no other than you.

With this realisation, it makes it easier to let go and forgive.

The way you let go and forgive is to forgive into love. You forgive into love because you acknowledge that your experience has come from love, for you.

Steps to let go and forgive into love:

Steps	Explanation	Example
1. Remember a person or moment where you were hurt	Bring back the memory of the event or person and what they did to you. Just remember!	The person who beat me up and caused me to have an emergency brain operation and learn to walk and talk again at the age of 22
2. Compassion	See that same person in front of you. Now: feel compassion for them. Think about who that person is. What pain or anguish could they have gone through in their life that made them do what they did Remember, "hurt people hurt people."	I saw the man who had put me in hospital and I tried to imagine him as a little boy in his childhood. Perhaps he came from poverty and had an abusive parent. Perhaps his life was a constant struggle and the only means of survival was for him to become who he was

3. Let go by forgiving into love	From a vantage point of compassion, we let go by thanking, forgiving and blessing the person. Acknowledge that what they did is a lesson for us from the universe. We do this by visualisation and meditation. You don't have to connect with the person and do this. But if you want to, and the opportunity exists, then go for it	I visualise thanking, forgiving and blessing the man who assaulted me. I see myself hugging him and saying I thank you for the lesson, I forgive you and I bless you for a life filled with health, happiness and love.
4. Learnings	Ask yourself 'what did I learn?' 'How did the situation make my life better?' Consider the lessons you could derive from the situation, painful as it might be. How did these lessons elevate you and help you grow?	I accepted the incident as a universal life lesson. It made me realise what I need to do. It opened my eyes to my talents and skill set. The reason I am here living life with purpose.

By letting go, the past no longer eats at you. Your personal history ceases to destroy you from the inside.

"Time isn't precious at all, because it is an illusion. What you perceive as precious is not time but the one point that is out of time: the Now. That is precious indeed. The more you are focused on time — past and future — the more you miss the Now, the most precious thing there is."

Eckhart Tolle

Method 2: Be the bubble

Here's a secret: there is a key to unlocking your life. The key represents the most important aspect of anything you are doing. Often, we forget, put off, or just don't do the things we are supposed to do. The key puts it all together. The key opens up whatever you need. The key reminds you that you have what it takes to do what you need to do. The key opens that closed door and takes you into a space in which you need to be.

But the key is not just one single thing. It is a culmination of everything you have been through ... and is used in the moment of your choosing. The key is to Be the Bubble.

Be the Bubble teaches us how to be present and to disregard all forms of unwanted feelings, pain and negativities. The method enables you to live in the moment and to experience what you need to experience.

Remember that the past, the current and the future all exist right now. By being the bubble you have to let go, living in the present aligned to who you are so that you can live your destiny.

We are all sentient beings. You absorb energy from people and events that you do not want to or need. You also live your life based on the perceptions you have and that you receive from the world around you.

We all need space, a place to breathe, to connect with ourselves and to be free in the confines of our own boundaries. This space is created and designed by you, for you, and is utilised by Being the Bubble.

Be the Bubble...

Imagine being in a bubble on a cloud floating above the world. You have a viewpoint of clarity of your past, your current and your future. The journey of your lifespan is in your view.

The present is you right now in this bubble. There is nothing else but you. It is you with just you. This is the first time you have ever experienced yourself in this light. It is you with just you. No coverings, no make up, no masks, no other energies, no forces, just you, naked!

You see yourself as a beautiful creature. You see your beauty inside and out. You begin to truly love yourself for the first time. You acknowledge that you are complete. You have everything you need to achieve what you came here for. You have what it takes to live your passions, to use your power, to make decisions for you, to live the life you are supposed to, the life you have always wanted, the life in your dreams, to live for you, to be magical, to share your light upon the world, to be successful, to be happy, to be you!

In this bubble, you have your human compass where you see your happy and enjoyable path to the future from the journey of your past. You see what you need to do and you become confident of who you are now. You have a humble confidence that lights you up and fills you with an energy from your source. You are grateful for the journey you have been on and everything that you have been through - the good, bad, ugly and gorgeous.

You are here now, happy, content, confident. You are a light and an energy because of every single thing that you have experienced.

This is the first time that you surrender to yourself. You are who you have always wanted to be and you now continue to fly on the wings that you have created.

You are in a place where the culmination of your past, your present and future is in your hands. Right now, you realise that the past, the present and the future is actually this current moment. It's one period, this period. It's yours and nothing nor no one can take this away from you. This is you! Right now! Forever and always!

You cease lamenting about the past.

You cease worrying about the future.

You are focussed on the present and you enjoy your life right now.

The future is yours. The future is now. It is what you are creating now. Right now you are happy, you are loved, you have gratitude and you are successful.

In this bubble you are immune to criticism and compliments. You are in complete control of everything that exists within your bubble. You can manage everything that occurs outside the bubble to best suit yourself within the bubble.

Your emotions are understood, acknowledged and dealt with accordingly. Your thoughts, speech and actions align with who you are, what you are here for, what you are fighting for and where you are going.

Your days are filled with optimism and you get what you need from everything that comes your way. You do not need anything from anyone else - you create your own magic.

You make decisions and live your life, doing what you need to do without any other energies coming into play. If people don't like what you do when you're being you, then that's fine. Good for them. Whether they love it or hate it, that is their response and it has nothing to do with you - except to give you an opportunity to turn the response into positive energy.

You have an appreciation of whatever comes your way. Whatever comes your way is meant to be there, for you to control and create magic with. You assess, learn and grow in the way that you should. You now elevate your world and everything around you.

Now...

Put it into your life. Be the Bubble wherever you are and in whatever you do. This transparent sphere contains only one thing. One awesome and brilliant thing - YOU!

This is your life and your opportunity to shine. By Being the Bubble you are the master of your emotions, reactions, creations and how you behave.

No one else knows about your bubble. That gives you power. It allows you to be your own leader.

Your bubble provides you with a safe place every second of every day. It allows you to not fight reality.

You are in your bubble, protected and guided by your personal values and beliefs.

What is, is. You see what is outside the bubble from a distance - with clear objectivity - without letting emotion control you. You define your thoughts, speech and action.

You recognise what is out of your control. Other people's shit is not your shit, which you have no responsibility for!

You acknowledge that the answers are always inside you. You know the answer for you and the decisions to take. Ask yourself, trust yourself and act with integrity and value.

You require no validation from anyone or thing around you. You understand that seeking validation from external sources is just another way of using your external world to make yourself feel better. You know that's just bullshit, a temporary illusion that gives your power away.

You will behave with complete sincerity to who you are - to yourself and to the world around you. It follows that you will not have any excuses, because excuses are bullshit that come from fear, not from being yourself.

Having an excuse is actually creating a worthless energy: 'I can't, I won't, I'll do it next year". All the other lies you tell yourself!

You will love yourself first by forgiving into love because you are aware that it has all come from love, for love, for you!

You will embrace and combat your fear. You will climb your mountain every moment you can! You will acknowledge that what you should have done was actually done because you are right here right now because of them. If the now is dark for you then now is the chance that you have been waiting for to create the light.

You will control and acknowledge your thoughts, speech and action. This is your power. You will use it to the best of your ability and create magic!

You will not judge others! Who the fuck are you to judge? You have neither understanding nor responsibility to judge others! Everyone has their own reason, meaning and purpose so let their shit be their shit. Only get involved when you can elevate them. By judging others you create the negative energy that you do not want in your life.

The way you communicate with yourself and others is now guided by an intuition of what your words can create and how they affect the energy you possess. What you say is what you mean. You trust yourself. Lying doesn't exist for you. You won't lie to yourself nor to others. Every word you think of and speak has a meaning that you choose because you know that it has the power that influences your circumstances.

Of course, you are still human. There will be moments that you just cannot handle. When you feel overwhelmed and just cannot take it anymore then the bubble will burst. That's perfectly fine; you will be okay. Just remember that when "bad things" happen it's for a reason, a meaning and a purpose. It will make you stronger and more capable.

In fact, the point of the bubble is actually for it to burst!

Life is all about how you rebuild your bubble. The vitality, the power, flexibility and strength of your fresh energy forms the new bubble!

It's like the moment just before you scream in frustration (or even in pleasure). You feel so much better after that scream. In fact, you become stronger, wiser, more ready and confident to take on what's in front of you.

To Be the Bubble to its fullest is to get to the point of the burst and then to recover and then build the bubble to its strongest and most flexible point every time. Just as the world changes and grows, so does your bubble and so do you.

A simple intervention is activated in that moment when your bubble bursts. It requires some breathing room for you to gather your thoughts, realise what made it burst and how to control yourself in the future. This space and time can be a split second or a few weeks. This is your world and you choose how you want to live and define it.

All you have to do is STOP! Close your eyes, breathe in slowly through your nose and out through your mouth. Connect to yourself at that moment and just be with every breath you take. Imagine the bubble reforming with a stronger and more flexible film and with revitalised energy.

Stress, panic, anxiety and negative emotions are effectively paying attention to everything except what's right in front of you. You have the power when you are in the present and within your bubble. This is when you create your future. This is the moment when all decisions are made. By taking a moment you are connecting to who you are so that you can get back to the path that you need to be on.

"You alone are enough. You have nothing to prove to anyone."

Maya Angelou

Method 3: Realising that you are enough

This method fuels you to create a remarkable future. It's about letting go of the past, living in the moment and not having concern about how people perceive you or what they expect from you. It is about you, climbing your mountain, your happiness, your values, your worth, your essence, your gut, what you are fighting for and where you are going. The fear that you once had of others has dissipated. You now embrace fear, expect nothing except stepping up, climbing and summiting your mountain.

Realising you are enough is a game changer!

We all think that we will be enough or a better person when we achieve something. Usually this something is absolute bullshit as it makes you no happier than you are at this present moment.

Do you think you will be satisfied when you lose 10 kilograms or get that 6 pack or make that million dollars or buy that house or drive that car or eat that meal? Not a chance! The truth is, you are enough right now.

You were enough the day you were born! You are enough with every breath that you take! You are enough every morning when you rise! You are enough every night when you shut your eyes! You are enough when you are asleep, irrespective of your dreams! You are enough now!

You were born for a reason, a meaning and a purpose. The day you were born is when the world needed you. Right now, the world needs you more!

All the blockages that you have, the feelings of unworthiness, your unloving self, the comparisons you make, the various perceptions you control, the attitude you hold, the fear you have and create, the choices and decisions you make, the consequences that you design, the trauma you hold onto and the life you choose to live ... all of that is coming together to form your life as it is right in this very moment.

You struggle to see the pathway to where you need to go. Your vision is blocked. Be the Bubble means having a mindset that incorporates all the discoveries so that you can let go of the past, live in the moment and realise that you are enough!

This method brings you back to who you are meant to be, by acknowledging that you are enough.

Just by being yourself you are enough! By being you, you will be happy and succeed!

There's a simple reason why you do not think that you are enough. It's because of the journey of your life up until this point.

Life as we know it makes you feel unworthy, unloved and not good enough; and because of this, you have had a mindset of fear and failure, of choosing incorrectly and creating the consequences that you do not want. All of these energies and mixed emotions make you feel unworthy and inadequate.

The way you were and are treated, mistreated, guided, mentored, shouted at, redirected, told you not good enough, should have done better or scored that goal, told to shut up, do this, do that, get hit or tackled, or challenged, how you got up, bounced back - the world's perception, and not your naked one, has made you feel inadequate.

Remember that this is because of you. Because you don't yet have the correct mindset.

None of it is done intentionally by anyone else. It has been created unintentionally by you! This is life; you cannot blame anyone for anything. The problem is simply that you don't realise that you are enough!

I know it's hard to hear, but you are responsible for your life. You have the responsibility to use these tools to transform, be happy, full of love and success and to uplift and elevate your world.

When you have a perception of happiness, love and success, your attitude is of happiness, love and success. Your thoughts, speech and actions are of happiness, love and success. Everything you have been through is an acknowledgement of happiness, love and success. That means there have never been failures and therefore you have no fear.

The three methods we looked at, have profound benefits for your financial, mental, emotional, spiritual, physical health.

An easy way to keep these three methods with you is to remember the following acronym

Be the Bubble - by realising you are Enough - and Letting Go (B.E.L)

Always ring your **BEL!**

"People often say that motivation doesn't last. Well, neither does bathing - that's why we recommend it daily."

Zig Ziglar

Discovery 6: Daily routines

We are all as strong - physically, mentally, spiritually - as we need to be. Although our strength is mostly tangible, the real power and magic is intangible. It's in our minds! We were born with a purpose and mission. Our strength is our responsibility to love and overcome what we face. The power is the courage to be exactly who you are without any fear to be you.

Everything in this book and everything in life is all a mindset and with the tools you've learned you can always choose to be positive.

Sometimes we feel shit and sometimes we feel good. But you have a choice. Your power and responsibility is to be positive! It is all about choices, after all.

Creating change in your life fundamentally involves taking responsibility. Instead of running away from your problems, search for the lesson in everything you go through. In each challenge and uncomfortable situation lies a message for you to make the correct choice about whatever you are facing. Be the Bubble gives you the correct mindset to live up to who you truly believe you are.

To get your mindset where you want it to be, is about your daily design and by putting what you need into practice. This provides discipline and focus. It creates the daily energy that you need. It allows you to live each moment how you should.

In any moment, you should always have the correct mindset so that your perception, decisions, behaviour, thoughts, speech and action are all aligned to who you are and where you are going.

We all need to find our own routine that gets us ready to make the day count. Ready to make the correct decisions and not allow negativities or emotions to control our actions.

Your routines must be aligned to your purpose and you should do them every single day. A fresh start with a clear, happy and focused mindset is where it is all at.

Your daily design does not have to look like mine nor anyone else's. Choose what you need to do to give you the balance and energy for your day.

My suggestion is to do it once every day, for no more than thirty minutes at a time. If you need it more frequently or for longer periods of time then go ahead. But what is important about your daily design is that you do it for just the right amount of time that you need and not a moment more. Often, when good things are done too much they become a burden and eventually are abandoned.

Choose a time and space that you are comfortable with to design your day. Acknowledge that this is a mindset that can be done anywhere at any time.

I prefer to perform my routine before I leave the house in the morning. Before my mind gets consumed from the daily grind of your life. Before I give my energy away to the news or social media. This energy will stay with you for the entire day. The more you do this the more connected and in tune you will be. Your daily design prepares you for your day so that everything is in alignment.

Suggested Daily Design:

Item	Duration
Upon waking up, as your eyes open say the following: • Thank you for another day. Another moment to live the life that I love. To be happy. To be me!	1 second
Meditate: • Sit on a chair or the floor, upright without any limbs crossing • Close your eyes • Breathe in deeply through your nose. Mouth closed. • Imagine positive energy coming in through your nose, down your throat and into your stomach. • Hold it there for three seconds. Positive energy and light will expand into every cell of your being • Breathe out slowly for four seconds and imagine all the negativities being removed from your body, mind and soul. • Repeat for at least 10 minutes.	10 minutes

Ring your BEL:
   • Let go by forgiving into love:
      ◦ Choose a memory, be compassionate, let it go by forgiving into love, take a moment to have gratitude for the learning.
      ◦ If there are no memories then let go of any negative emotion, concern, stress or anxiety you are currently feeling.
   • Visualisation of Be the Bubble:
      ◦ Form your bubble and connect to who you are with all the discoveries in alignment
      ◦ Think about:
         ▪ Perception vs attitude
         ▪ Love yourself first
         ▪ Only success - no failures or mistakes
         ▪ It's all about choices
   • I am enough Affirmations
      ◦ Look at yourself in the mirror and say the following three times each with meaning and emotion:
         ▪ I am enough!
         ▪ I am beautiful!
         ▪ I am strong!
         ▪ I love you!
         ▪ Thank you for being you!
         ▪ I am going to have the best day!
	5 minutes

Purpose Journal:
   • Write a to do list to achieve your goals today
   • Write down 3 things that you are grateful for
   • Write down 3 points of what could be better today than yesterday
   • Write I love you
	5 minutes

Do some form of activity. Exercise / walk / stretch / yoga / pilates	10 minutes

The daily design will get you ready for your day and align you to where you are going. You will be you every step of the way, without letting emotion interfere with anything you face. You will think, speak and act the way you should. Your day will be happy and successful.

If every day is happy and successful then your life will be happy and successful.

"Life is a culmination of the past, an awareness of the present, an indication of a future beyond knowledge, the quality that gives a touch of divinity to matter."

Charles Lindbergh

TO BE THE BUBBLE

To piece all discoveries together is to Be the Bubble

To Be the Bubble is to live a life that you have always dreamt of. It is living your dream right now. Not in the future for some specific achievement.

The only thing that you have to achieve is to Be the Bubble.

When you are the bubble, you perceive what you see and experience in a way that defines the attitude that you walk with. It is how you behave and the energy you possess every moment of every day.

This gives you the opportunity and capacity to love yourself first.

Loving yourself first is your most important mission in this life. If you can't fully accept yourself, you'll never find true happiness, even if you have fame and billions in your bank account. You'll constantly be seeking something that will make you feel better but that only ever provides a temporary fix which, in my opinion, is the main cause of addictions and obsessions.

When you love yourself first, you will have the mindset and acknowledgement to realise that everything that happens to you - "mistakes", "failures", "problems", etc. is actually not happening to you but for you - from love, for love! You will now take everything that happens to you as reason, meaning and purpose all for you to succeed.

You will now embrace your fears and summit your mountain every step of your way. This will give you a success mindset and this is how you will live - successfully!

Don't worry if you don't reach the top immediately. The truth is, there is no top. Once you summit your mountain, a new vista opens in front of you. As you grow and learn - as you reach the peak you are heading to - you reach a more profound point of understanding, and you want to grow more. Each peak reveals a new, more brilliant peak. Life is a constant process of ascending to ever greater heights.

When you set your focus on your purpose, when that peak is your true happiness, then the journey itself is a joyful process. You proceed through life proactively. With purpose. With joy.

This will allow you to surrender to yourself and now you will be mindful about every decision and choice that you make, the choices that come to you because of them and the consequences that you create.

You can now let go of the past, be the bubble in every moment, realise that you are enough right now.

You now live your destiny in this moment right now full of happiness, full of health - financial, physical, mental, emotional, spiritual with complete success. All the crap in your head - thoughts of pain, confusion, damage, expectations, negativities and everything that causes you to not live life in a productive, efficient and successful manner will be eradicated

The cause and reason of this book is for you, your family, your friends, your colleagues, your business partners and your enemies to create and live the best life that can be lived and in turn create light in this world.

When there is light, specifically when you create it, is when there is a clear vision, a focus on doing your bit in this world for you to achieve your true success. With this you will intrinsically do good for good and shine light wherever you are.

Let's uplift this world we live in.

I'm in!

Are you?

ACKNOWLEDGEMENTS

For the ones that really stick out, here is a special acknowledgement:

- To my friends who were with me that night at the club and who rushed me to hospital. If they had not rushed me to hospital or reacted with any aggression or any differently than how they did then I would certainly not be here.

- To Sunninghill Hospital that was led by the client liaison officer Pip Kruger. Pip treated my supporters, family, friends and strangers like her own family. She made halls out of unavailable spaces for people to pray for me in unity. Without her, the power of prayer may not have been realised and I may not have been here.

- To the nurses who were and still are angels in this world we live in. Nurses dedicate their lives to help, clean up and save other people's lives. Extremely special people that often do not get the praise that they deserve.

- To my inimitable neurosurgeon - Dr. Marouzio Zorio and trauma surgeon - Dr Leslie Maurice Fingleson. Dr. Zorio fixed my brain and even though the prognosis was poor, always connected with my family and gave them hope and comfort. He looked after and guided me for three years in a time when I needed him the most. Dr. Fingelson saved my life the moment I arrived at the hospital. He removed the vomit from my lungs immediately to stop me from drowning and got me ready and stable enough for Dr. Zorio to work on my brain.

- To my parents, Mark and Michelle Silberman who were the strength that pulled everything and everyone together. Their belief in me when I was down and literally out and their belief in me now, will always hold a special place in my heart.

- To my brother Ryan and his wife Lauren who had my back and always will. I know this hit Ryan hard. Harder than anything. Even to this day.

- To my boys, Noah Leo and Jaxson Levi who are my current heroes.

- To my beautiful wife, Tandi-Lee who is my life's greatest achievement.

ARTICLES & PICTURES

By LIESL VENTER and SAPA

A 22-YEAR-OLD man was yesterday fighting for his life after a savage beating by bouncers at a Rivonia nightclub hours earlier, apparently because one of his friends was black.

Bradley Silberman was in a stable but critical condition yesterday afternoon following surgery for severe head injuries, said Sunninghill Hospital spokesman Pip Kruger.

Mr Silberman and his four friends were all allegedly assaulted by the bouncers, but only he was critically injured.

He was admitted to the hospital in the early hours of yesterday morning.

Ms Kruger said Mr Silberman had undergone brain surgery shortly after being admitted to the hospital.

Asked if the operation had been successful, she said: "It's difficult to say at this stage.

"All I can say is that he is in a stable but critical condition."

According to Johannesburg police spokesman Sergeant Sanku Tsunke, the man and his four friends had visited the Tiger Tiger Club in Rivonia.

They were kicked out allegedly because "one of their group was black".

Sgt Tsunke said police could not confirm if the assault on the five was indeed a racial confrontation, but this was under investigation.

"It appears they were kicked out by the bouncers, who then allegedly set off after them."

Sgt Tsunke said no one had yet been arrested in connection with the case.

Police have appealed to witnesses to come forward with information so that the suspects may be arrested.

Inspector Jones Baloyi can be contacted on 083-514-0641.
– lieslv@citizen.co.za

HEADLINE IN THE CITIZEN NEWSPAPER 14 NOVEMBER 2004

ZAPIRO COMIC IN THE SOWETAN NEWSPAPER - 18 NOVEMBER 2004

Hold thumbs for 'Beef'

Oliver Roberts

It's a tragic example of Brad Silberman's humility that his parents didn't realise just how many people loved him until he was lying in a coma at Sunninghill Hospital.

Mark and Michelle Silberman have been totally overwhelmed by the number of friends who have come in during the week to see their son. Many are from the Jewish community and when a prayer service is held each evening in the hospital's reception, more than 150 attend.

"We knew Brad was a special guy but we had no idea what an effect he'd had on so many people," confirms Michelle. "A little boy came in the other day with a balloon and a card for Brad. I had never seen him before - it turned out Brad is his rugby coach."

Among the other well-wishers have been former primary and high school mates, past headmasters and fellow Wits University students, including the entire rugby team. "Even his sports master from Standard 5 has come by. How do you react to that? It's incredible," says Michelle.

In the short time the *Chronicle* was at the hospital, several friends visited. Some left a few minutes later. Others sat quietly in chairs, reading to pass the hours.

"Brad has an incredible soul. We have guards who patrol the area where we live and he often invites them in to the house to teach them how to use the computer. That's the kind of man he is," explains Mark.

According to older brother Ryan, Brad, or "Beef" as he is affection-

Mark and Michelle Silberman with a picture of their son, Brad (22), who sustained brain damage after being beaten by a bouncer outside Tiger Tiger club in Rivonia.

ately known, is a problem solver, the guy everyone goes to when they're feeling down. He's also a mediator, a trait which indirectly led to the incident outside the Tiger Tiger club in Rivonia last Sunday where he was beaten by a bouncer.

"The attack was totally unprovoked," states Mark. "At the time it happened, Brad had his car keys in his hands and was ready to drive away. Brad always did all he could to avoid conflict."

Mark and Michelle say during the past week they have received many calls from people who've

had similar experiences with bouncers. Michelle in particular has vowed to let this be the last time something as terrible as this happens.

"I just want it to stop," she says. "My mission is to get night club security regulated and controlled."

At the time of going to press on Monday morning, Brad's condition had improved. According to Sunninghill Hospital's spokesman, Pip Kruger, Brad was starting to wake up and was responding to basic commands. He was still on a ventilator.

Second bouncer arrested

A second bouncer was arrested on Friday in connection with the incident outside Tiger Tiger club in Rivonia. In the incident, Wits student Brad Silberman (22) was beaten so badly he is in hospital with brain damage (see separate story). The suspect (20) appeared in the Randburg Magistrate's Court and was released on R2 000 bail, to appear again with a fellow suspect (29) on December 15.

They are facing charges of assault with intent to cause grievous bodily harm.

The investigation continues.

**HOLD THUMBS FOR BEEF IN THE SANDTON CHRONICLE
19 NOVEMBER 2004**

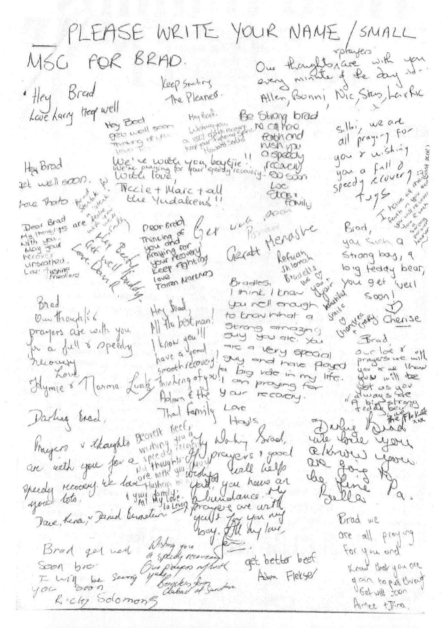

LETTER OF HOPE OUTSIDE HOSPITAL. THIS IS 1 OF MANY

family ... Bradley Silberman with his mother Michelle and brother Ryan.

PIC OF ME, MOM AND BRO DURING RECOVERY TIME

Club-beating victim's recovery 'a miracle'

By Shaun Smillie

Just two months after 22-year-old was bashed into a coma, he is well on his way to a miraculous recovery

Two months ago Bradley Silberman was at death's door, deep in a coma. Today, family and doctors are calling his recovery nothing short of a miracle.

"The trauma surgeon is amazed at the progress Bradley has made," said Silberman's mother, Michelle.

"He said he thought Bradley would end up doing nothing more than blowing bubbles in the corner."

Silberman was savagely beaten outside a northern suburbs nightclub last November and spent weeks in hospital in critical condition.

But even with his miracle recovery, it has been a rough ride for the 22-year-old.

He is back home now, but as his mother puts it: "He has to start his life all over, bit by bit."

This entails a painful and frustrating routine of rehabilitation sessions, visits to physiotherapists, occupational therapists and even speech therapists.

It's during these sessions that Beefy – as he is affectionately known to his friends – draws on the inspiration of his sporting hero, cyclist Lance Armstrong, who also had to go through rehabilitation sessions during his battle against cancer.

Silberman, his family and friends are still trying to piece together their lives following the events that took place during the early hours of November 14.

The previous evening had started out in a celebratory mood when Silberman and his friends set off to celebrate a friend's birthday at the Tiger Tiger nightclub, in Rivonia.

Hours later, in the club's carpark, Silberman and his friend Bradley Seweitz were allegedly beaten up by bouncers said to be members of the Elite Security Group, a shady organisation reportedly linked to other vicious attacks on club patrons in Johannesburg and Durban.

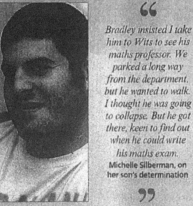

> Bradley insisted I take him to Wits to see his maths professor. We parked a long way from the department, but he wanted to walk. I thought that he was going to collapse. But he got there, keen to find out when he could write his maths exam.
>
> Michelle Silberman, on her son's determination

A witness to the fight that night said Silberman was punched twice in the face and hit his head on the concrete kerb when he fell to the ground.

Silberman sustained brain damage and was admitted to Sunninghill Hospital in a coma. He underwent brain surgery.

For days it was touch and go. Family and friends kept vigil at his bedside praying that he would wake.

Then slowly Silberman began to show signs of recovery. One day his brother Ryan was sitting by his bed willing him to wake.

Ryan asked his brother to squeeze his hand if he could hear him.

"He did. It was the best feeling. It was amazing," Ryan said.

Silberman still has no memory of that night outside Tiger Tiger.

"When I woke up, two of my friends were by my bed. I said to them: 'Where am I?'" Silberman recalled.

While Silberman was in hospital, his brother set up a website in his honour.

"We were amazed at the response, people have e-mailed from all over. We were touched," said mom Michelle.

The website is full of good-will messages, from friends and even people who had only briefly met Silberman or who learned of his plight through the media.

One such message came from a well-wisher who sent a dedication from Australia, claiming that he had played in a rugby match against Silberman five years ago.

On Christmas Eve, Silberman was discharged from hospital.

His injuries have left him with impaired vision.

He finds it hard to concentrate, the once strong and fit sportsman tires easily and he has had to learn to walk all over again.

His poor eyesight means that he can't drive anymore and watching TV is impossible.

Worst of all, Silberman can never again indulge in his first love – playing rugby.

"I guess I will have to look at other sports, maybe squash," he said.

Michelle Silberman remains angry over the attack on her son. "Do you know that the owners of Tiger Tiger have said they would pay for Bradley's medical expenses?

"We haven't seen a cent. They haven't even sent a letter of apology," she said.

Ironically, Silberman does receive promotional SMSs from the nightclub, promising free drinks.

While his mother is angry, some of his friends who were with him on that fateful night have been traumatised by the event and have sought counselling.

But Michelle Silberman believes her son's determination will eventually pull him through.

His father Mark wrote on the website how Silberman, on his fifth birthday, had promised to give up carrying around his security blanket and to stop sucking his thumb. And from that day on, he had kept his word.

Now Michelle has another story of Bradley's determination that she likes to tell.

It happened a few days ago.

"Bradley insisted that I take him to Wits to see his maths professor.

"We parked a long way from the department, but he wanted to walk. I thought that he was going to collapse. But he got there, keen to find out when he could write his maths exam."

Silberman was suppose to have written the exam two days after he was beaten up at Tiger Tiger.

Now he plans to write the exam in February.

His doctors say he can't do it. But Silberman is not listening.

He has already got a study plan.

■ ssm@star.co.za

Miracle boy 'Beef' is back

Oliver Roberts

Michelle Silberman had never before understood the power of prayer until her son Brad woke from a coma and began to speak.

Brad was admitted to Sunninghill Hospital during the early hours of November 14 last year. He had severe brain trauma after being allegedly beaten by a bouncer outside a Rivonia night club.

Following emergency surgery, Brad remained in critical condition for weeks. The neurosurgeon explained Brad's brain had swelled to such dangerous proportions it had slowly begun to shut down.

Every day, the hospital's reception area was filled with people from Brad's present and distant past. Family, friends, teammates he'd lead on the rugby field, past headmasters and even a little boy he'd coached in rugby - some came once, others every night, a few never left, but all of them prayed.

Then Brad woke up.

"He's a miracle child," says Michelle. "All the doctors agree his recovery has been miraculous - they have never seen anything like it. I now have no doubt it's because of all the prayers, no doubt at all."

Though in a far better mental and physical state than the initial tentative prognosis stated, many aspects of Brad's life have changed irrevocably. Once a proficient sportsman, he is having to learn to walk again and his vision is impaired - he cannot drive or watch television - and he gets tired very quickly. However, his condition is improving.

"It's going to be a slow process," Brad admits, contemplating months of treatment, including occupational, speech and hearing therapy. "I'm not angry about what happened, just frustrated, but I will get back soon."

On the night of the incident, Brad - or "Beef" as he is better known - had gone out to the Tiger Tiger Club to celebrate the end of his studies at Wits University. Now, because he missed a final maths exam, he may have to repeat the year unless he can write a supplementary exam in the next couple of weeks, something he will struggle to do.

Brad has no recollection of the events that night, but is concerned that something like this could have happened. "Just as a CEO is responsible for his staff, so should the owner of a club take charge of the people he employs," he says, referring to the two bouncers, allegedly members of the notorious Elite group, who were arrested a few days after the incident.

The owners of Tiger Tiger Club eventually contacted the Silbermans and have offered to cover the medical costs. They have also invited Brad to host his next birthday party there, all expenses paid.

"As a family, we are all very grateful and thank God every day that Brad is still with us," says Michelle. "Ryan, Brad's brother, has been brilliant. When Brad first got home, Ryan would help to bathe him and wait outside the door if Brad went to the bathroom. It's been wonderful to see such love between two brothers."

Beef's interpretation on this whole event is the kind of philosophy which has made him such a well-liked guy. "I have always had a strong faith, but maybe this happened because God wanted to show me something more. If you believe in God, all that something like this does is make you more spiritual."

Club-beating victim Brad Silberman has amazed doctors with his recovery.

MIRACLE BOY BEEF IS BACK IN THE NEWS- FEBRUARY 2005

Beaten by bouncers at nightclub, he's now on the way to miraculous recovery

BY SHAUN SMILLIE

Bradley Silberman has taken the next big step in his recovery – he has left home.

Eight months ago, doctors thought 22-year-old Silberman would spend the rest of his days in a vegetative state after he was beaten up by bouncers outside a Rivonia nightclub, Tiger Tiger.

Today, Silberman was due to fly to Israel and Greece for four weeks on his own.

He has been given the okay by his doctor, and the reluctant approval from his mother, Michelle. Talking about it is enough to bring tears to her eyes.

"Even when he just goes out at night, I worry. This month is going to be the hardest, but it is something he has to do."

Silberman has gone to Israel to watch the Maccabi Games, where Jews come from around the world compete against one another every four years. Shortly before he was assaulted, he had been selected to play rugby for South Africa at the Maccabi Games.

On the mend ... Bradley Silberman is going overseas.

While Michelle might be apprehensive about her son's trip, Silberman is looking forward to it, although a little nervously.

A couple of months back, the consensus was that Silberman wouldn't be able to drive a car again. He was suffering from tunnel vision and there was a concern that he could have seizures while behind the wheel. Now his sight is back to normal and he is driving.

Many of his therapy sessions are also coming to an end. However, his mother says there is still a long road to recovery. Part of that road is dealing with the psychological scars of the accident. Silberman's memory of the accident stopped shortly before he entered the nightclub.

"I remember driving to Tiger Tiger, looking across at a friend, and that was it," he said.

There may be no memories, but Silberman had to overcome fears of being in open spaces and of being with crowds of people.

Once Silberman returns from his overseas travels, his next big step is to study. The plan is to do a B Comm degree in entrepreneurship through Unisa.

He will have a little help, as his brother Ryan wants to study with him. But before all that, Silberman's mother has scribbled her last concerns over his trip in a note she has left for him to read on the plane.

The note tells him to listen to his inner voice, so that it can keep him out of trouble. It is also this inner voice, she believes, that has acted as a guiding light to his miraculous recovery.

ssm@star.co.za

ON THE WAY TO A MIRACULOUS RECOVERY IN THE STAR - 7 JULY 2005

WEDDING PIC (OF ME AND TANDS)

FAMILY PIC

TO LIFE, TO NETCARE SUNNINGHILL HOSPITAL

The ten year anniversary of a courageous journey to healing was celebrated at our hospital. It was no ordinary journey and the survivor was no ordinary patient. What began all those years ago as an innocent night out, ended tragically in the Netcare Sunninghill Emergency Department after a club bouncer had beaten the young man to a pulp. While the story was recounted in newspapers and on television, Bradley Silberman fought for his life in ICU. The doctors and nurses had saved his life; the rest was up to the power of prayer and Bradley's determination. The young 22 year old, recovering from head and multiple injuries, left the hospital only to return ten years later as a healthy strapping, grateful young man. Bradley Silberman wanted to give back. He returned on his anniversary, laden with gifts for every nurse in our hospital. An end to an amazing story, one which he will never forget, nor will over 500 of our nurses who received his hampers.

10 YEAR NURSE ARTICLE - 14 NOVEMBER 2014